SABOTAGING
THE
WORLD
CHURCH

by Dr. Jack Van Impe

Jack Van Impe Ministries
P.O. Box 7004 • Troy, MI 48007-7004
In Canada: Box 1717, Postal Station A
Windsor, Ontario, N9A 6Y1 Canada

ISBN 0-934803-83-8

CONTENTS

Foreword

A Tribute to
Dr. Van Impe's New Position on Love

by Dr. Robert Savage
Missionary in St. Croix, Virgin Islands

Back in the 1930s and 1940s, my dad—H. H. Savage—was known as "Mr. Fundamentalist" for the state of Michigan. He courageously and effectively led the battle for fundamentalism. But if Dad were alive today, he would be called by many a "compromiser." His guilt would be that he cooperated with pastors and churches of many denominations in Union Lenten services (Detroit), evangelistic campaigns and Bible Conferences. I call these who would discredit Dad "neo-fundamentalists." They are not historic fundamentalists because they have added so much to what was originally the position of fundamentalism.

Jack Van Impe's magnificent article, "That They All May Be One," is, in a sense, a call to return to historic fundamentalism and be rid of the fighting, the extremism and the misguided views of the "neo-fundamentalists."

Back in the 16th century, Martin Luther was used of God to bring multitudes back to the teaching of the apostles. I pray that Jack Van Impe might be used in this last part of the 20th century to bring multitudes back to a position of love for each other and oneness in Christ.

Preface

Many men of God feel led to ignore their critics. I have done so during the last ten years. Now the hour has arrived for me to state my position for a number of reasons:

1. The leading of the Holy Spirit.
2. To keep a movement from destroying itself. Fundamentalism began as a grand and glorious organization to uplift the Lord Jesus Christ and defend Christological truth centering around His deity, virgin birth, substitutionary atonement, and bodily resurrection. Presently, however, many of our leaders have become sidetracked. They now judge men and movements on the basis of a leader's likes and dislikes. These personal preferences are based upon man-made rules and regulations rather than the Word of God. If such prejudices against good and godly men continue, fundamentalism's decline and fall will be swift. Jesus said, "A house divided against itself cannot stand" (see Mark 3:25).
3. To save the forthcoming generation of ministerial students the heartaches and pitfalls I encountered by following fallible men rather than the infallible and inerrant Word of God.
4. To correct the rumors and allegations released by the leaders of neo-fundamentalism against hundreds of precious brothers in Christ who have been misjudged, mislabeled, and misunderstood.

—Dr. Jack Van Impe

Introduction

There are 20,780 denominations worldwide according to a news release in *Christianity Today*. The majority of these groups proclaim a strict allegiance to the doctrine of Christ.

The millions joined to these multitudinous groups are, according to God's Word, "one body in Christ Jesus" or, literally, members of the true world church. The reason any one denomination differs from the other 20,779 is usually some secondary truth that is non-consequential to salvation or the fundamentals of the faith. Though Christ repeatedly prayed for unity as verification of His mission, still too often human beings feel that battling for prejudiced, man-made interpretations is more important than obeying Christ.

In 1984, I wrote a book entitled *Heart Disease in Christ's Body*. At that point in my life, I dealt with scores of negative issues, reports, letters, and personalities. That era of my life is past. My battle against religious tyranny has toppled the majority of extreme militants. Thus, I re-edit my book, leaving out some 200 pages of negative experiences and bring it to date by proclaiming hundreds of positive declarations concerning the unity of the body of Christ, the world church for whom Jesus suffered, bled, and died.

Tragically, the unity for which the Saviour pleaded is too often abused by those who claim to love Christ the most—the so-called orthodox defenders of the faith. These leaders claim to accept the fact that all brothers are members of the body of Christ, yet they refuse fellowship with any who disagree with them over any issue, however insignificant.

The resulting prejudice, bitterness, envy, and evil thinking are symptoms of the dreadful and destructive disease afflicting the hearts of all those who practice such unloveliness, as well as the very heart of Christ.

Our Lord prayed for UNITY often in John 17. He desired that every member of His body would function in a coordinated and harmonious manner. Today, every member of Christ's body is to endeavor *to keep the unity of the Spirit in the bond of peace* (Ephesians 4:3).

Presently, the multitudinous voices proclaiming and printing bigoted statements against those attempting to obey Christ's command to love and live in unity prove that "heart disease in Christ's body" is out of control. Proverbs 6:14 pictures the condition: *Frowardness is in his heart, he deviseth mischief continually; he soweth discord.*

The only solution is the Word of God. Let the Holy Spirit use His sword and scalpel to perform the greatest bypass surgery ever—changing each and all from walking in the flesh to abiding in the Spirit—from carnality to spirituality. When this operation has been completed, healing will return to Christ's body.

Chapter 1

Fundamentalism's City-wide Crusader

This chapter is adapted from my biography, "They Call Him the Walking Bible," by my longtime friend, Roger Campbell.

It is the final night of the crusade, the culmination of months of planning and prayer. The crowd is arriving and the chatter of voices provides cover for the choir to rehearse its selection one more time. Those who have found their places early in order to enjoy the preliminary music strain to hear over the scuffing of feet and the buzz of conversation all around them.

In rooms beneath the stadium bleachers there is another kind of conversation going on as hundreds pray for this closing service. They are the counselors, pastors, committee people, and others who have given of themselves to make all this happen.

Some who are making their way down the crowded aisles searching for seats will never forget this week. Their lives have been changed.

They feel as if they have come to the end of a long search. Others are still searching.

A man escorts his wife down the stairs and to the row of chairs nearest the speaker's platform. They have decided to make one last try before divorce. It will be their night.

A teenage boy clutching a new Bible moves up the steps to the top row in the stadium.

Ushers assist an older gentleman in a wheelchair. He has been bitter about life since the accident that caused his paralysis. He had been on his way to a dance, hoping for some vicarious enjoyment in seeing others move about so freely, when the stadium sign attracted his attention and caused him to have his driver bring him to hear "The Walking Bible."

As pastors and workers emerge from the prayer rooms, there is a quieting of the crowd. Eyes follow Dr. Van Impe and Rexella, his wife, as they join others who have platform responsibilities in this crusade finale.

Tonight's message will be prophetic, and everything in the service builds toward it. There is an expectant air in the crowd. They have been looking forward all week to this explanation of Bible prophecy as it relates to world events. Many have brought friends and relatives whose curiosity has been aroused by the timely topic.

First-nighters eye the evangelist as the service develops. They see a man who has a burden, yet is human enough for a quick smile. He seems both distant and approachable. Immersed in thought, yet alert to everything around him.

Dr. Van Impe's part in the musical portion of the meeting provides many in the audience their first opportunity to hear the accorgan, an instrument that blends the benefits of both the accordion and the organ. His ability as a musician is established quickly. He is totally involved. A perfectionist.

The bond between this husband-wife team is too strong to be hidden. While Rexella is communicating with the crowd in testimony and song, the man in her life beams approval. And well he might. He knows her ministry in music is no performance, and he respects the work of God through this lady so loved by crusade congregations around the world.

When the evangelist rises to preach, there are mixed feelings throughout the stadium. There is anticipation of hearing the awaited prophetic message, but it is accompanied by a touch of sadness at this being the last message Dr. Van Impe will deliver to this audience.

Regular attenders are not surprised at the army of Bible verses marshalled to explain and prove each point of the sermon. They've come to expect it. Many feel as if they have been bathed in the Bible during these meetings, and the cleansing effect is showing in their lives. Old wrongs have been made right...bills paid...

questionable practices dropped...dedication renewed.

Newcomers are overwhelmed by the avalanche of inspiration. They have never heard this much Bible in so short a time. They are amazed at the evangelist's ability to quote the written Word of God. It is evident that his aim is to place his own personality in the background and confront his hearers with an ultimatum from the Almighty. He seems to desire to be only a voice, forcing his audience to grapple with the Word.

In this setting and atmosphere, the results are predictable. Conviction grows. Sin seems more sinful. The cross and Resurrection appear in their proper biblical perspective. Conversions take place. Backsliders return. The faithful are refueled. The fire spreads. Blessings abound. The following reports highlight the excitement of the crusades as crowds build and souls are saved.

In Indianapolis, 12,000 gathered for the closing service of the crusade. Hundreds were converted. It was a cold week for outdoor meetings, yet thousands gathered nightly, wrapped in blankets to hear "The Walking Bible."

Over 10,000 attended the final night in Dayton, Ohio. It was a week of great spiritual victories with many decisions for Christ.

"Crusade Crowds Larger Than Any Sports Gathering in the History of Hershey, PA" was the headline in the news release reporting that great crusade. The attendance set a record for any religious gathering in that part of the state.

Portsmouth, Virginia, responded so well that closed-circuit TV was used to accommodate the crowds. There were 600 conversions.

In Syracuse, New York, 1,000 came forward at the invitation. The Scranton, Pennsylvania Crusade resulted in the largest attendance since the days of Billy Sunday.

In Honolulu, Hawaii, thousands attended the service at the internationally famous Waikiki Shell, and 500 were converted, along with thousands of restorations and rededications. In the Panama Canal Zone, the crowds were so large that it was necessary to move the meetings outdoors.

Churches in the Philippines hosted a crusade in January 1975. One of the high points of this effort was the response of the pastors. Special seminars on soul-winning were scheduled for them by Dr. Van Impe, and resulted in a pledge to try to win 10,000 souls during that year. Decisions for Christ totaled 6,514, and the ministers won the additional 10,000, making it one of the most fruitful of Dr. Van Impe's ministry.

Ten million people attended the mass city-wide endeavors, and 500,000 decisions for Christ were registered.

Presently, the mass city-wide endeavors in

stadiums, coliseums, and ball parks have ceased. Sad, but true. Nevertheless, historians will one day record that Dr. Jack Van Impe conducted the most city-wide crusades of the twentieth century, with the exception of Dr. Billy Graham.

Who or what caused the disintegration and demise of such dynamic, Spirit-empowered crusades which produced tens of thousands of decisions for Christ?

In the chapters that follow, Dr. Van Impe shares firsthand his call to the ministry and personal experiences in city-wide crusades—including the opposition and pressure brought to bear upon him by the leaders of the so-called "neo-fundamentalist" movement (a term coined by Dr. Carl McIntyre). It is a story of heartache and pain inflicted by those who are driven by a spirit of inquisition against all who fail to conform to their narrow and rigid obsessions. In the tradition of the self-righteous, hell-raising Pharisees (the term used by Dr. John R. Rice), this group has ridden roughshod over all other believers in vengeful fury, wrapping themselves in a soiled and tattered banner of Christian separatism.

Chapter 2
The Call of God

My Belgian parents arrived in America in 1929, the time of the Great Depression. They came seeking fame and fortune, but ended up in the deepest of poverty for the first five years of their lives as immigrants in this great land.

Since my father, Oscar Van Impe, was a talented accordionist, he sought employment as an entertainer in order to supplement his income as an automobile factory worker. Before long, he became a nightclub favorite among the 40,000 Belgians who lived in the city of Detroit. When I was but eight years of age, he had me appearing before the same crowds with a miniature accordion.

As a result of his constant nightclub associations, Dad started to drink heavily, and the years that followed became a nightmare in our home. Then, after ten years of a living hell upon earth, the Spirit of God began to do a deep work within the hearts of my parents.

One holiday weekend, I decided not to accompany Mom and Dad to the nightspots to entertain. I promised them I would be home by 9:00 p.m., but decided to stay out as long as I desired, thinking they would never know. At 11:00 p.m., a car, traveling at a tremendous rate of speed, struck me as I was crossing an intersection. My body was thrown thirty-five feet through the air. Immediately, the half-drunken occupants of the speeding vehicle stopped, looked at me, and decided to stuff my body into the trunk. Fortunately, a detective who was passing by saw what was occurring, stopped the proceedings, and arrested the culprits.

Though my body was badly bruised, there were no serious complications. God, however, used this accident to open the minds and hearts of my parents to the reality of death and eternity.

Soon afterward, my father trusted Jesus Christ as his personal Saviour. Then Mom made the same commitment. I was shocked. God had given me a new father and mother. They were born again and completely changed by His mighty power. At that point, 2 Corinthians 5:17 became a living reality in our home, *Therefore if any man be in Christ, he is a new creature: old things are passed away; behold, all things are become new.*

My heart was so overwhelmed by the change in my parents that I, too, wanted to be saved. We had lived across the street from a small, gospel-preaching church for years. In fact, I had often raided this godly group of people with rotten tomatoes in earlier days. The following Sunday morning, I boldly walked into the church, announced my need of the Saviour, and was led to Christ before Sunday school even began. What joy filled my entire being as I became a new creation in Christ Jesus. I made my public profession of faith at the end of the morning service, and a few months later, submitted to baptism, publicly declaring my faith in the Lord Jesus Christ.

My conversion took place during my high school days and, as a teenager, I had but one desire—to wholeheartedly follow Christ. I wanted to go to Bible college so badly that I could hardly wait for graduation day. I longed to begin devouring God's Word.

At the time of my salvation, I was such a raw pagan that I did not even know the story of Jonah and the whale. I had never heard John 3:16. In fact, my ignorance of God's Word was so great that I thought an apostle and epistle were husband and wife!

Bible college days

Imagine my shock when I arrived at Detroit Bible College and heard such mind-boggling terms as "theology," "hermeneutics," "exegesis," "apologetics," and "Greek." I was petrified. I did not know the meaning of "soteriology," "pneumatology," or even such simple phrases as "the deity of Christ," and "the substitutionary atonement." Nevertheless, I was determined to know Christ in a greater way through

His blessed Word. And study I did—settling only for an "A" average.

Shortly after beginning college, I began appearing on television with Dr. Robert Parr and "The America Back To God Hour." I also traveled extensively as a musician with the Voice of Christian Youth (Youth for Christ in Detroit). These activities kept me busy in the service of the King until my graduation from college.

Just prior to graduation, I was ordained to the gospel ministry at the Christian Fellowship Tabernacle in Marine City, Michigan. The examining council was composed of eleven minister: Dr. A. G. Kruschwitz, Rev. Earl Linderholm, Dr. W. S. Hottel, Rev. L. P. Buroker, Rev. Albert Ludwig, Rev. John Pinches, Rev. Harrey E. Cochenour, Rev. Orrin Van Loon, Sr., Rev. Orrin Van Loon, Jr., Rev. Harold Moran, and Rev. William Reiter. The council chairman was Dr. W. S. Hottel, a noted Bible scholar and writer.

I had prepared diligently for the great night when I would be questioned orally for two hours by this panel of godly brethren. For weeks, I had tucked 500 Bible verses into my head and heart through memorization. When I gave my doctrinal statement, I quoted verses in machine-gun fashion to back up each point. I actually used the majority of the memorized portions in my presentation. Upon finishing the task, Dr. W. S. Hottel commended my usage of God's Word.

The Fundamental Fellowship, a Michigan religious periodical, reported my ordination under the heading: "Jack Van Impe Ordained to Ministry Following Unusual Ordination Council." The subtitle read: "Only One Question Asked Following Doctrinal Statement." What was that question? Dr. Hottel, the chairman of the council, voiced it: "Jack, do you really believe what you have just told us you believe?" I replied, "Yes sir, I certainly do, with all my heart." Dr. Hottel responded by saying, "Gentlemen, we have another Martin Luther on our hands. Let's ordain him."

I can only praise God for His goodness in helping a lost young pagan (who had never heard John 3:16 prior to his salvation) to reach this point in his Christian life in just five short years. After observing the power of God through His Word during this ordination council, I determined that I would complete my memorization program by storing every verse of the New Testament in my head and heart. The project took seventeen years to complete, but I reached the goal that the Spirit of God had burdened me to attain.

Now I was on my own, conducting rallies and concerts for Youth for Christ. One night in Pontiac, Michigan, I met a young lady named Rexella Shelton. She was to sing on the same program where I was speaking. When I saw her, it was love at first sight. Then, as she gave her testimony and mentioned that God had called her into evangelism, I knew this was it. Six months later, I asked, "Wilt thou?" It was a hot, summery night and Rexella wilted. Praise God!

The Lord certainly knew what He was doing when He joined in holy matrimony two individuals who would conduct 800 full-length, local church crusades and 253 mass, city-wide endeavors over a period of 32 years. Because we were faithful in the smallest churches in earlier days, God gave Rexella and me the largest crusades ever conducted under the banner of fundamentalism.

Today, I am as committed to affirming and upholding the position of historic, biblical fundamentalism as I have ever been. Still, I am deeply burdened over the divisiveness espoused by those who call themselves "militant fundamentalists." As I deal with this issue and tell my story in the remaining pages of this book, I shall do so honestly and factually. Because 10,000 fundamentalist pastors have sponsored my city-wide crusades, I know this movement as well as any human being alive.

May I say at the outset that the majority of our fundamentalist leaders are great men of God whose hearts are filled with a love for others. They would gladly lay down their lives to lift the fallen and bring sinners to Christ. Most of them love their brothers in Christ as well and are as broken over the present infighting as I am. I have received hundreds of letters telling of the heartaches, frustrations, and disappointments these men are presently experiencing because of a small, vocal minority who believe that one is compromising if he is not constantly attacking others. Unless this group, which I call "neo-fundamentalists," is labeling and mislabeling others in the most crude language, they feel they are not defending the faith. How wrong when men feel there is inherent virtue in conflict, criticism, ostracism, and suspicion. How wicked when men believe they constitute a very exclusive group which holds a monopoly on truth and righteousness and constantly adds new names to its "blacklist" as others fail to meet their qualifications and standards. I thank God for the silent majority who believe Christianity is still based on the premise of love and who attempt to practice and preach it as God's norm for believers. In earlier days, this spirit of inquisition was not present. How joyous it was to serve the Lord in the local churches and city-wide endeavors during that time of interdenominationalism.

Years of blessings

Because of the love between brethren, the blessings of God overflowed in our crusade services. During more than 800 local church revivals, Rexella and I saw every attendance record shattered in all but ten of our meetings. God was mightily upon the scene, visiting us with genuine revival, week after week.

In one church where an invitation had never been given and where the pastor had never pushed for conversion, the entire church membership walked the aisle for salvation or a public profession of their faith. The situation was startling, to say the least.

During our meetings in both Warren and Detroit, Michigan, God visited us with such Holy Spirit conviction that the membership stayed to pray and confess their sins until 4:00 p.m. on the Lord's Day. They hardly had time to get home and return for the evening service. Hundreds were saved.

Repeatedly, we saw the power of God unleashed in 800 local church crusades conducted from 1948 to 1969. At that point in time, we were faced with an important decision in our expanding ministry. Rexella and I had received over 1,500 invitations to conduct local church endeavors. Were we to give each of them an eight-day meeting, we would be scheduled for the next sixty years!

Because of this situation, as well as the opportunity to reach multitudes more for Christ, we made the decision to begin conducting mass, city-wide crusades in 1970. These powerful meetings united local, Bible-believing churches for great outreaches which took place in arenas, ball parks, and coliseums. God again smiled upon our decision to unite believers and reach the lost. Doors began opening faster than we had anticipated, and we were faced with many exciting challenges.

The results of these crusades, reported in the opening chapter, tell the story of some of the most thrilling days Rexella and I have ever experienced in our service for the King.

Threats

In the midst of such blessings, of course, Satan was displeased. He wanted to end this ministry. He often used threats of death to try to disrupt the joy and blessings we experienced as thousands were saved and revived.

We went to the Panama Canal Zone just after revolutionaries had taken over the university there. The threats by Communist sympathizers were many. The climate was electric, and tension was at an all-time high. Still, the response to our crusade was tremendous. In fact, the crowd grew to such proportions that we were forced to meet outdoors. There were hills all around me, and yet I stood in the open, preaching on Ezekiel 38,39—the great prophecy of a cataclysmic war between Russia and Israel! A sniper on a hillside could easily have shot me, but God gave me the confidence to preach with conviction and power, and I was not afraid.

It was the closing Friday night of our Kansas City, Missouri Crusade when I discovered that my life was in jeopardy. As I was announcing the subjects for the final two evenings, I saw a dozen policemen enter the building. One of the officers walked to the platform and whispered, "We have every exit covered because we have received official reports that there is a plot to kill you."

For the next forty-eight hours, Rexella and I were unable to travel without armed guards. Neither handshaking nor Bible-signing was allowed until the final night of the crusade and, even then, only with officers present.

I recall that, before the police came on the scene just preceding the service, a man rushed up to me, asking for help in the prayer room immediately. Since there were only four minutes remaining before the start of the service, I told him he would have to wait until after the message. He walked away, cursing. Perhaps this was the key move in the planned assassination. Only God knows, and He is always on time in protecting His own.

We learned later that three men were involved in the plot. Because a number of drug pushers had been converted, the narcotics traffic was disrupted. Therefore, three ringleaders decided that the "troublemaker" had to go. Fortunately, they did not succeed in their murderous venture. Rexella and I arrived home safely. We continue to give thanks to God for His protection.

Hershey, Pennsylvania, was another danger spot. The crusade crowds were especially responsive and attendance soon climbed to 10,500. Revival was in the air! Then, in the midst of this blessing, a note threatening my life was discovered in the offering plate. The writer promised to kill me if I preached my announced message topic, "A Politician's Greatest Blunder," the next evening. The phone in our motel room rang incessantly throughout that night. To make matters worse, the calls were not coming through the switchboard, but were being dialed from other rooms. Masked men attended the meeting the next evening. Yet, once again, the providence of God kept us from harm.

Another deliverance from death came during our Bicentennial Crusade in Philadelphia in 1976. I shared the experience with our friends and supporters via the Bicentennial/Anniversary issue of our *Jack Van Impe Crusade Newsletter:*

Praise God, from whom all blessings flow! God graciously protected the city of Philadelphia, America's 200th birthday celebration, the Bicentennial Crusade, and my life. Instead of violence, blessing occurred the week of July 4 through 11.

The Congressional Record, F.B.I. files, *Reader's Digest* and the *Herald Tribune* (international English news-

27

paper), had all carried warnings concerning the planned violence which might have destroyed Philadelphia and the Bicentennial activities. Communists and militant supporters had mapped out a program in Chicago, January 30 through February 1, 1976, to bring "fireworks" to the "City of Brotherly Love" on July 4.

In addition to these reports, I had personally received warnings. I was told that militants wanted me "out of the way."

July 2, Rexella and I left home for Philadelphia. As we stood in the foyer of our home praying, my heart was heavy. I felt that I might not return. I had said nothing to Rexella about the mail I had received.

That same morning, my staff had given me a note. It said, "We are praying that God will bring you back to us safely." Every staff member had signed it. Being a man, I fought my emotions, but was deeply moved. I knew God had a plan, and all I wanted was His will.

The evening of July 2 was spent in Philadelphia. Three truckloads of militants arrived in front of our hotel and marched past with the clenched fist salute of the Communist movement. On television, radicals were being interviewed. They boldly boasted of the way they would dynamite the city on July 4. I wondered how the TV media could be so calloused as to allow these revolutionaries thousands of dollars worth of air time.

The fear could be felt in the air. Millions who had planned to come to Philadelphia stayed away. The downtown hotels were forty to fifty percent vacant, although they had been completely booked months in advance.

On our opening night, fifty of the sponsoring churches believed it best to conduct their own services, in order to avoid any violence. Police filled the city, and I was told that the militants were under complete surveillance as plainclothesmen infiltrated their ranks. Six guards were assigned to the crusade platform. My personal bodyguards demanded that I wear a bulletproof vest. I tried it the first night and felt handicapped. The next day, I said, "Men, I have spent the night in prayer and feel it is a lack of faith to wear this vest for the entire crusade." From that moment onward, perfect peace filled my soul.

The 500,000 who came to Christ during our years of city-wide evangelism made all the heartaches and threats worthwhile. Yet, in the midst of the blessedness of serving the Lord and seeing all that He was doing through the crusades, my heart began—slowly and almost imperceptibly at first—to be deeply troubled at the inconsistencies and injustices I saw. Often, for example, the basic values of honesty and integrity seemed to be lacking in those who thought themselves to be the most committed to righteousness. The threats of death I could take. Dishonesty and hypocrisy I could not.

It is amazing to me that men who pride themselves on being men of strong convictions and firm principles can be so insensitive to what is truly righteous. In Florida, the local pastors organized a committee and elected a chairman. He was a godly man, committed to Christ. However, he had been in an accident several years earlier and had a disfigured ear. For cosmetic reasons, he allowed his hair to grow long enough to cover the deformed ear. His hair wasn't long, but it did cover his ear. Consequently, several of the crusade participants felt that this brother's hair was a sign of compromise. As a result, they withdrew from the crusade, thereby forcing its cancellation. They also refused to pay the substantial bills they had already incurred, though they previously agreed to honorably meet their commitments. Ultimately, our organization absorbed these costs. Sad, isn't it? The men who had canceled the crusade because of their so-called "convictions" about hair conveniently overlooked the principle of honesty concerning their bills. They also lost an opportunity to reach thousands of lost souls in their area for the Lord.

I confess that I do not understand the mentality that permits a person to rationalize away what is clearly sin in the name of avoiding that which is questionably "compromise." These men were like the Pharisees of Christ's time who strained at gnats and swallowed camels (see Matthew 23:24). During the decade I spent in city-wide crusades, I saw so much of this kind of behavior that I came to expect it. Yet I never ceased to be saddened by it, and I began to wonder how long I could continue working in such an environment and still expect God to bless my labors.

Chapter 3

Separation Without Sanctification

In 1973, we conducted a city-wide crusade in Chicago's McCormick Place. I had a new car with only five hundred miles on it and, since I did not need it for the week, I left it parked in the lot. When I picked it up at the end of the week, I gave my claim check to the parking attendant, and off he went to get the car. While I was waiting for him to return, I became engaged in conversation and did not notice the vehicle when the attendant drove up in it. He got out, handed me the key, and said, "Have a nice day."

When I entered my automobile, I was startled. The windshield was gone and the entire front-end was smashed. The man who had parked it earlier in the week was a drug user. Knowing that I would not return for a week, he had used my car, gotten into an accident and demolished the front end. Then, the attendant who returned my car to me had the audacity to act as if nothing had happened, even to the point of telling me to have a nice day!

The latter attendant's total disregard for what was so obvious reminds me of the attitude of many neo-fundamentalists. In fact, from this point onward, I will use the term "neo-fundamentalist" to designate an unscriptural movement within true fundamentalism that would rather fight than switch.

Neo-fundamentalists seemingly ignore what the Scriptures say about love and unity among Christians and present a lopsided view of what constitutes orthodoxy. They preach and teach a misinterpreted message on separation, and then view themselves as the only ones who understand such truth. They are like the parking lot attendant who handed me the keys to a demolished car and nonchalantly said, "Have a nice day."

Perhaps the single most significant element of neo-fundamentalism is the emphasis given to ecclesiastical separation. Militant separatists go to unbelievable extremes to ensure that their associations are "pure." Some are so consumed with a passion to separate from others who differ with them over non-important issues that it becomes an obsession with them. I have known more than one man who broke fellowship with so many others that, ultimately, he was left completely isolated, feeling that he was God's sole spokesman in the city where he ministered. Neo-fundamentalism is filled with this kind of Pharisaism. Elijah, in his day, told God that he stood alone. God rebuked his foolish servant by stating in 1 Kings 19:18, *Yet I have left me seven thousand in Israel, all the knees which have not bowed unto Baal, and every mouth which hath not kissed him.* Today there are tens of thousands who stand for historic fundamentalism's principles but who are, nevertheless, rejected simply because they do not dot their "I's" or cross their "T's" in accordance with a self-appointed leader's inconsequential regulations.

Holy blackmail

This passion of neo-fundamentalists that drives them into isolationism and demands the same of their followers has led to a climate of fear, suspicion, and underhandedness, as they attempt to force others into their unscriptural mold.

In fact, neo-fundamentalists frequently use threats and blackmail to accomplish their wishes in manipulating others. This happened to me on a number of occasions. The method of operation is disgustingly simple. It begins as leaders turn brothers against one another by mislabeling them under various titles as compromisers. Then those suspected of fellowship with the alleged compromisers also become guilty. The suspected are then warned by telephone or letter to immediately break fellowship with such tainted brothers or suffer the humiliation and agony of being publicly exposed as defectors. Imagine the mentality involved in such reasoning and also the fear it induces as men, trying to save their ministries, succumb to such pressure tactics.

The other method of public exposure involves the neo-fundamentalist scandal sheets, which usually copy one another's rumors about brothers in Christ. These small papers are nothing more than gossip columns produced under the guise of "defending the faith." They contain the latest "uncovered compromise" of alleged pseudo-fundamentalists (fakes) or supposed new-evangelicals, who are one rung down the ladder. Since Christians are forbidden to go to law against believers, the slander is never retracted via an apology if proven wrong.

Do such inquisitions and scandal sheets hurt the reputations of God's servants? Unfortunately, yes. Some Christians are ready to believe virtually anything they hear or read. Few bother to investigate or write the accused for verification of the innuendoes and rumors slandering him.

On trial

During my latter years in city-wide endeavors, pastors who had heard such allegations often questioned me at the inception of a crusade. I would usually meet with them on Monday afternoon to answer the numerous charges about my fellowship with some good brothers in Christ who had also been mislabeled. At times, the sessions would last three or four hours before the men were convinced that the religious gazettes were erroneous in their presentation of the facts or that they had purposely stacked the evidence against solid men of God. Frequently, the same question resurfaced years after an issue had been settled. Needless to say, the hours of questioning were exasperating and emotionally draining. By crusade time, I had neither the enthusiasm nor the joy necessary to do my best service for Christ under such judgmental circumstances.

Why did I allow such trials to occur? Simply because I wanted to be a fundamentalist. Consequently, I did everything within my power to correct any misunderstanding created by the neo-fundamentalist media machine. As a result, I continued bowing to men, thinking this was the way to please God. But I grew exceedingly frustrated in my attempts to please men with such condemnatory mentalities. My spirit became grieved at being forced to break fellowship with accused brothers in Christ whom I loved dearly in the Lord. They were giants for God, holding to the principles of historic fundamentalism. Nevertheless, I was forbidden fellowship with them because an autocratic leader disliked them.

My Holy Spirit-directed conscience would not allow me to continue under such unscriptural practices. A burden to air a declaration of my views of love for all the brotherhood began building in me. I knew that I must one day reveal publicly what God's Spirit was creating in my heart.

Senseless criticism

The attitudes held by many people we met seemed to be senseless in the light of the Saviour's command to love one another. For instance, Rexella and I conducted a crusade in Honolulu, Hawaii, in 1980. We decided to combine a tour group from the states for the event. Tours are open to the general public. As a result, many of God's dear people from numerous denominations went with us. A militant fundamentalist pastor in Hawaii discovered this and, on the final evening of the crusade, was backstage at the famous Waikiki Shell. Victory abounded as scores came forward for salvation. We were so short on counselors that I began dealing with the souls personally. This was difficult in that I had just taped a one-hour television special and still had additional taping that needed to be done. The crew was waiting. Nevertheless, souls came first. While dealing with a broken sinner, I heard shouting. Guess what! I had an angry pastor on my hands. He discovered that one of the tour group members was a Pentecostal. Thus, he could be heard ranting, "This ministry has compromised by allowing a Pentecostal to join the tour group." Imagine the confusion generated as precious souls were turning to Christ. This temper tantrum was certainly out of harmony with the command of Jesus, who said in John 13:35, *By this shall all men know that ye are my disciples, if ye have love one to another.* Again my spirit and conscience informed me that there had to be something wrong with such prejudiced thinking. This was not historic fundamentalism which originated among brothers of multiplied denominations. This was something new and wrong. It was the seed of neo-fundamentalism beginning to sprout and flourish.

Runaway separation

There was more to separation than ecclesiastical isolationism. Neo-fundamentalism also practiced racial separation. They went hand in hand. Blacks were usually conveniently excluded by simply stating, "Blacks are not fundamentalists." How well I remember the heartache I experienced when, in Maryland, two black pastors came to me in tears, saying, "Do you really expect God to bless this lily-white crusade?" That statement took root and I never forgot it. How hypocritical we are when we send missionaries to Africa and then refuse to fellowship with black brothers in Christ in America.

In all my years of evangelism, I had two integrated campaigns. On the final night of the Philadelphia Bicentennial Crusade, a neo-fundamentalist racist came from out of state to see for himself if I was guilty of all the compromise reported to him by informers. The local crusade leaders, fearful that they too might be labeled as compromisers, told the black sponsoring ministers that they would not be seated on the platform or be recognized as on previous nights. I knew nothing about the situation until black leaders shared the information with me later. Imagine such bigotry in the name of the God of love. Forgive us, Lord, for our hypocrisy.

Denominational separatism also became popular. Although historic fundamentalism had always been interdenominational, many of today's fundamentalists excluded other fundamentalists who had different denominational tags. As a case in point, two precious men of God whom I met and with whom I fellowshipped at the interdenominational World Congress of Fundamentalists in Scotland were excluded from my crusade in Tennessee, a few months later. Why? They were not Baptists. Had I insisted that they be included, the sponsoring pastors would have canceled the crusade. Still, two godly brothers were grieved that one group of fundamentalists accepted them while another group rejected them.

By the mid-1970s I began growing weary of trying to please the militant factions within the movement. By 1977, I was consciously grappling with the question of whether or not I wanted to continue being identified with the judgmental mentality of neo-fundamentalism—not historic fundamentalism, but radicalism. Thus, I preached a message of unity at the Sword of the Lord Conference on Soulwinning and Revival at Cobo Hall in Detroit. Repeatedly, in the sermon, I stated that I could no longer conduct city-wide crusades in an atmosphere of suspicion, disunity, and hatred. I pled for a new love among the brethren. Did it work? Following my message, the rumor sheets announced that I had "renounced fundamentalism" at Cobo Hall. This was totally untrue.

Soon there was little hope of ever seeing another crusade where love abounded. The bitterness grew, fighting flourished, and suspicion reigned. No one would again be able to make a move of any kind without being accused. Informers increased. New victims were added to the blacklist. In spite of this situation, I continued city-wide crusades for another three years. The meetings, however, began to deteriorate noticeably. The rumor mill was succeeding. The infighting it caused robbed us of former blessings. Whereas hundreds had been saved in each meeting during previous years, we were now fortunate to see a handful of converts. Without the manifestation of love visible among the brethren, what could we expect?

Chapter 4

Children Sitting in the Marketplace

In one church where Rexella and I conducted a crusade, the pastor's three-year-old son was present in all the meetings. He especially liked the music. He had never seen an accordion before. It so fascinated him when I did the bellows shake on this instrument that he went home and tried to imitate me. His father told me about it, and I related the story to the congregation. This little fellow, after hearing me discuss him, said to his father, "If that evangelist makes one more remark about me, I'm quitting the church."

Such an incident is humorous when a three-year-old child is involved. It is not so funny when a grown man acts this way. How interesting is the fact that Jesus compared the Pharisees to children. *But whereunto shall I liken this generation? It is like unto children sitting in the markets, and calling unto their fellows, and saying, We have piped unto you, and ye have not danced; we have mourned unto you, and ye have not lamented* (Matthew 11:16,17).

I have often discovered neo-fundamentalists to be similar to this biblical description. They are like children who throw temper tantrums when they do not get their way.

In North Carolina, for example, the pastors of the two largest churches involved in my crusade were at each other's throats the entire week. One even came to me and said that he was actually praying for the death of the other. If God answered, the work of the Lord would then be done properly throughout the area. What a climate for revival!

Similar attitudes among ministers would either make or break a crusade. If the men were unified, loving, and supportive, the blessings of God were innumerable, as multitudes flocked to the Saviour. If, on the other hand, the pastors were fighting and fussing, the crusade was drastically hindered.

The problem was usually jealousy, not doctrinal purity. When we were considering a crusade in Lynchburg, Virginia, a group of local pastors informed me that the campaign would not be considered unless Jerry Falwell was excluded. Their motivation was the green-eyed monster of envy. Because I felt that such pettiness could not be honored, I refused their request, and the plans to reach this area with a great unified effort were canceled.

A tragic spirit of divisiveness also occurred in Pennsylvania. A local pastor, chosen as the publicity agent, became extremely embittered at the crusade's success. He said to me, "I preach better than you do—still, I can't fill my church. Why do these people want to come and listen to you? Why do they fill this huge auditorium nightly?" Needless to say, Satan had won the victory. Demonic power took over. Three times during the week, people were removed from the auditorium bodily, screaming obscenities. What I felt was frightening, and the meeting ended as a disastrous reproach to the cause of Christ.

In Alabama, we were looking forward with expectation to a wonderful crusade. Upon arrival at the auditorium, a pastor met me, threw his arms around me, and tearfully said, "This is a victory. For years I have prayed for a Jack Van Impe crusade in our city." By Tuesday night, however, he had become involved in a ruckus with another pastor and childishly cried, "If I can't have it my way, I'll take my buses and go home." He did. I never saw him again. I wonder what he told his members.

On other occasions, I actually observed ministers fighting publicly backstage over decision cards. How often leading preachers, looked up to by thousands, became like children. That God blessed some of these meetings at all is solely because of His abounding grace.

Small-minded legalism

One of the most troubling aspects of neo-fundamentalism was the extremes of legalism that were often espoused. One crusade sponsor refused to support the endeavor unless I submitted a written statement that none of my employees wore wire-rimmed glasses. He felt they were an indication of "hippyism." Other standards were set for choir members, counselors, and ushers. Rules governing makeup, hairstyles, clothing fashions, and accessories were among the regulations demanded by some of the legalists. Pastors not in agreement usually remained silent so as to keep peace.

How wrong such unscriptural separation is. There isn't a verse in God's Book that commands us to separate from a brother over hair length or clothing fashion. There are, however, scores of texts that order us to break fellowship with anyone practicing immorality in thought, word, and deed (study 1 Corinthians 5:9-11, Ephesians 5:3-12). If we based our separatist stance on God's Word, a lot of childish isolationism would cease.

In Green Bay, Wisconsin, we were closing our crusade on Sunday afternoon. The arena we were using featured wrestling on Sunday night, and then Rex Humbard was scheduled to begin a meeting on Monday. Humorously, the marquee outside the facility read:

Jack Van Impe

Wrestling

Rex Humbard

That might have been true of Jack Van

Impe at one time. However, during my remaining years in the ministry, I want to glorify God by being an example of His love—striving to promote true Christian unity among all members of His body.

I regret the years I spent bowing to the wishes of a few judgmental men. By accepting the platform of militant neo-fundamentalism, I consigned myself to their disgruntled ranks and forfeited fellowship with some wonderful men of God. Now, when I fellowship with men of like precious faith whom, through fear, I had kept at arm's length, I find that they are brothers deeply committed to God. They love the same Lord and preach the same message. Most of all, while holding to the true fundamentals of faith, they are not afraid to practice biblical love and unity.

In coming to the end of the line with militant radicalism—not historic fundamentalism— I have found a freedom in the Spirit that I had forgotten was possible.

Several months ago, I spoke with the pastor of a large church in Michigan. This pastor is a great historic fundamentalist who, like myself, has recently come out of the militantism. As we spoke, his comment to me was, "Jack, do you know what it is like to be **free**?"

I knew exactly what he meant.

Chapter 5

Defending the Faith in Love

GOD IS LOVE (1 John 4:8).

This is the message of Christianity.

LOVE brought Christ to earth. Jesus said, *I am come that they might have life, and that they might have it more abundantly* (John 10:10).

LOVE sent Him to the cross. *Hereby perceive we the love of God, because he laid down his life for us* (1 John 3:16).

LOVE made Him willing to die a sacrificial death by the shedding of His blood, *Unto him* [Christ] *that loved us, and washed us from our sins in his own blood* (Revelation 1:5).

THIS LOVE WAS FOR THE UNLOVE-LY—you and me. *Christ died for the ungodly* (Romans 5:6). Because of His love for us, we can gratefully say with Paul, *Thanks be unto God for his unspeakable gift* (2 Corinthians 9:15).

Has His love touched you?

Again, I say, GOD IS LOVE. It is part of His nature; one of His attributes. This nature becomes ours when the new birth occurs. When one becomes a new creation in Christ Jesus (see 2 Corinthians 5:17), he partakes of the DIVINE

NATURE (2 Peter 1:4). LOVE, then, is the hallmark, the evidence, the proof of a genuine salvation experience.

By this shall all men know that ye are my disciples, if ye have love one to another (John 13:35).

He that saith he is in the light, and hateth his brother, is in darkness even until now. He that loveth his brother abideth in the light, and there is none occasion of stumbling in him. But he that hateth his brother is in darkness, and walketh in darkness, and knoweth not whither he goeth, because that darkness hath blinded his eyes (1 John 2:9-11).

Beloved, let us love one another: for love is of God; and every one that loveth is born of God, and knoweth God. He that loveth not knoweth not God; for God is love (1 John 4:7,8).

If we love one another, God dwelleth in us (1 John 4:12). *If a man say, I love God, and hateth his brother, he is a liar* (1 John 4:20).

As one grows in grace, walks in the light, and seeks the filling of the Spirit, the intensity and immensity of love increases. When the Spirit of God is in control, one can begin to understand and practice the command of Jesus in Luke 6:27,28, *love your enemies, do good to them which hate you, bless them that curse you, and pray for them which despitefully use you.*

No one can do this apart from the Holy Spirit. That's why there is so little love evidenced among brethren these days! You see, it is not difficult to fake spiritual gifts, **but the fruit cannot be imitated**: *love, joy, peace, long-suffering, gentleness, goodness, faith, meekness, temperance* (Galatians 5:22,23). What a revival would break forth if men could see real Spirit-empowered Christianity in action! Instead, they see or hear about our "religious scandal sheets" which tear good Christians to shreds through articles by little men with big, jealous hearts.

Beloved, this is not the work of the Holy Spirit but rather of another spirit—the same spirit that made Cain envious to the point of slaying his brother and caused Saul to seek David's life. Yes, it is the spirit of him known as the *accuser of the brethren* (Revelation 12:10). Paul felt his attacks often. Sad to say, the attacks came through "ministers of Christ"—Paul's brothers in the faith who allowed themselves to be so used (see 2 Corinthians 11:23).

John, the disciple closest to the heart of Jesus, also knew the bitter pangs his brethren could inflict. He said, *I wrote unto the church: but Diotrephes, who loveth to have the preeminence* [be number one] *among them, receiveth us not. Wherefore, if I come, I will remember his deeds which he doeth, prating against us with malicious words: and not content therewith, neither doth he himself receive the brethren, and forbiddeth them that would, and casteth them out of the church* (3 John 9,10).

51

Sound familiar? Diotrephes is still present in the form of those who excommunicate, or attempt to destroy by written or spoken slander, fellowship with any brother who has shaken hands with the third cousin of an imagined compromiser. It's a good thing the original Diotrephes did not possess a printing press and mailing list, or he would have smeared Christ's favorite apostle in his "religious gazette!"

Beloved, don't follow this type of leadership. It bears all the earmarks of carnality. Galatians 5:19-21 lists the works of the flesh. Among them are, *hatred, variance, emulations, wrath, strife, seditions...envyings* [and], *murders* (vss. 20,21). All these terms are related to fighting. Immediately following this listing, verses 22,23 say there is a BETTER way—the FRUIT OF THE SPIRIT, which is *love, joy, peace, longsuffering, gentleness, goodness, faith, meekness* [and] *temperance*. Follow the leader who follows Christ (see 1 Corinthians 11:1). Look to the man who possesses love, gentleness, and meekness of spirit. He will be easy to find. His life and ministry are ones of reconciliation. He obeys all the Book, including Galatians 6:1, *Brethren, if a man be overtaken in a fault, ye which are spiritual, restore such an one in the spirit of meekness; considering thyself, lest thou also be tempted.*

As a layman, where do you stand? Do you look to men? Do you argue with your friends as to which leader is the greatest "saber rattler" of the faith? Are you, in effect, saying, *I am of Paul*, or *I am of Apollos*? If so, you are carnal (1 Corinthians 3:4). Do you rejoice when one of God's servants is defamed by another? Do you eagerly await the next edition of "*Religious Rumors*" to read the latest "scoop" on some brother in Christ? Do you delight in a brother or sister's heart being crushed through the poison pen of a carnal leader? The Spirit-filled believer [weeps] *with them that weep* (Romans 12:15).

Every born-again Christian, within many denominations, is a member of the body of Christ (1 Corinthians 12:13). When one member of that body is injured, the true Christian feels the hurt. *Bear ye one another's burdens, and so fulfil the law of Christ* (Galatians 6:2).

I can identify with many of my brothers who have felt the pangs of being publicly roasted by militant warriors. Three years ago, I preached a message on love at a Sword of the Lord Conference on Soulwinning and Revival. Never did I realize what problems a message on love could create. If you want to avoid being labeled a "pseudo [fake] fundamentalist" or a "compromiser," don't preach on love. This automatically brands one!

Since that day, article after article has attacked both my position and my character. **My position is: "I will love all of God's blood-bought children. I will refuse to accept the** false labels placed upon good, godly men by those who, like Diotrephes, want preeminence and glory, and who try to force their unscriptural convictions upon all believers under the threat of expulsion."

Don't accept the man-made labels placed upon good and godly men simply because an envious leader misbrands them.

My experience has been a blessed one. It has made a new man out of me. I, too, lived in a state of negativism. I also found fault and wrote hard letters. Then, after reading about myself in a 35-page release that could be purchased for $5.00 (to support a ministry of defamation), I sat back and, for the first time in my life, said, "Thank you, Lord." Why? First, because I could rest in Christ, even under attack. Secondly, because I had no desire to defend myself against the petty allegations concerning "secondary separation."

It was charged that I should not use a particular broadcasting company to get my message to the world because two good brothers whom the militants had labeled as "neo-evangelicals" also used the company. (I wonder what I would have had to do if we shopped at the same supermarket?)

Finally, I said, "Thank you, Lord" because He had delivered me from being like these embittered men whose entire ministries are based upon spying out the liberty which we have in

Christ Jesus (see Galatians 2:4). It must be a horrible experience to spend one's life in such unprofitable pursuits. Romans 14:10 states, *But why dost thou judge thy brother? or why dost thou set at nought thy brother? for we shall all stand before the judgment seat of Christ.*

All of us hold certain men in admiration. First, I desire to be like JESUS, *Who, when he was reviled, reviled not again; when he suffered, he threatened not* (1 Peter 2:23). Yea, I long to be like Spirit-filled Stephen, who, when he was being crushed to death by angry mobs, cried, *Lord, lay not this sin to their charge* (Acts 7:60).

My former pastor, Dr. G. B. Vick, was undoubtedly one of the greatest leaders of fundamentalism in the twentieth century. I dined with him on numerous occasions, became his friend, and had one of the greatest crusades of my entire ministry under his sponsorship. Still, in all our time together, I never heard him utter an unkind word about another brother in Christ. Dr. Vick is now with the Lord. How I miss his love, his counsel, and his example.

I also conducted four individual full-length crusades under the direction of Dr. Lee Roberson. Though I spent hours in his presence, I never heard criticism emanate from his lips. Once I saw him get up and walk away from a table where several ministers were slandering another brother. He said, "I don't have to listen to this." Thank you, Dr. Roberson, for the example you have set. I have never read a negative word about any man in your weekly paper. May the Lord raise up 10,000 fundamentalist leaders like you.

Defending the faith in love

Defending the faith in an unloving, vitriolic manner does not please God. Paul said, *and though I give my body to be burned* [as a martyr], *and have not charity* [love], *it profiteth me nothing* (1 Corinthians 13:3).

Many of the warriors are going to be shocked when they stand before Christ at the Judgment Seat. Think of it! They will receive no rewards though they DIED in defense of the faith. That's right, defending the faith in a vengeful manner produces no crowns because hatred, variance, wrath, strife, and envyings are of the flesh (see Galatians 5:19-21).

Love is so important.

Love covers a multitude of sins (see 1 Peter 4:8).

Love makes us to forbear one another, *endeavoring to keep the unity of the Spirit in the bond of peace* (Ephesians 4:3).

Love constrains us (see 2 Corinthians 5:14).

Love is of God, for God is love. Strife, envy, and hatred are not Spirit-instilled qualities. God himself speaks: *For whereas there is among you envying, and strife, and divisions, are ye not carnal, and walk as men?* (1

Corinthians 3:3). *From whence come wars and fightings among you? come they not hence, even of your lusts that war in your members?* (James 4:1).

For where envying and strife is, there is confusion and every evil work. But the wisdom that is from [God] *is first pure, then peaceable, gentle, and easy to be entreated, full of mercy and good fruits, without partiality, and without hypocrisy. And the fruit of righteousness is sown in peace of them that make peace* (James 3:16-18).

I can no longer remain silent. I must preach on the grievous issues that are causing heartache in the body of Christ. Remember that love and all the verses in this message are also part of the Scriptures and doctrine which must be defended (see 2 Timothy 4:1,2). If the angels aren't weeping over the present situation, the saints should!

Let's follow the footsteps of Jesus, our Saviour. Then let's follow leaders who live and act as though the love of God has been shed abroad in their hearts by the Holy Ghost (see Romans 5:8).

LOVE THE BROTHERHOOD (1 Peter 2:17).

Chapter 6

That They All May Be One

Why I Discontinued City-wide Crusades

The Lord Jesus, in His high priestly prayer, said, [Father], *as thou hast sent me into the world, even so have I also sent them into the world. Neither pray I for these alone, but for them also which shall believe on me through their word; THAT THEY ALL MAY BE ONE; as thou, Father, art in me, and I in thee, that they also may be one in us: that the world may believe that thou hast sent me* (John 17:18,20,21).

The unity or oneness of the family of God is the purpose of the Lord's prayer. Imagine! God in the flesh prayed that all Christians in all eras of time might have love for one another, as a sign that the Father really sent the Son and that Christianity is genuine. Is it any wonder that Jesus said, *By this shall all men know that ye are my disciples, if ye have love one to another* (John 13:35)?

We fundamentalists have often shied away from this text on oneness because of its constant use by the perpetrators of the one-world church—

but should we discard the baby with the bath water simply because an opponent has used it? Never. Such a position is woefully wrong when one considers that the desire of the Saviour's heart is that all genuine believers—past, present, and future—be united in love. Since we are to be *doers of the word, and not hearers only* (James 1:22), we soothe our consciences by convincing ourselves that the oneness for which Jesus prayed is realized and fulfilled solely through loving believers within our own denominational affiliation. How wrong! This is only the tip of the iceberg.

First Corinthians 12:13 declares, *For by one Spirit are we all baptized into one body*. This is not a Baptist, Nazarene, Pentecostal, Wesleyan Methodist, Christian and Missionary Alliance, or Evangelical Free Church body. Rather, it is the one body of Jesus Christ, composed of all born-again believers found in numerous denominations. Oh, if the church of Jesus Christ would quit sporting its labels and begin exalting the Saviour, calling themselves by His name—Christ or Christians—then love for one another would become the effectual force it was meant to be within the evangelical scene. It's too bad that God, who chose us and called us to salvation (see Ephesians 1:4) did not do it through one denomination. This would have made unity much simpler.

Do you really think denominational tags are

that important to God? In approximately 950-1100 A.D., the following evangelical groups existed: the Petrobrusians, Henricians, Arnoldists, Humiliati, Waldenses, Taborites, Lollards, and Bohemians. Where are they today, denominationally? Extinct! No one, except church history buffs, even recognizes their names. Nevertheless, they were all powerful groups similar to our modern-day denominations. They often ostracized and broke fellowship over secondary differences, just as denominationalists do today.

Picture mentally a future scene—the entrance of believers into glory at the Rapture. Can you envision them running to those who have been there for centuries and inquiring, "Were you a Henrician? An Arnoldist? Would you tell me if the Waldenses were greater separatists than the Lollards?"

What am I saying? It's simple—the only meaningful label in eternity will be "Christian." If Christ tarries another 500 years, the majority of today's labels will also pass away—but Christ and Christianity will live eternally!

Don't misunderstand. We may each have our personal convictions and hold to our doctrinal distinctives. Still, should we shun other brothers in Christ who disagree with our position? Could it be that most of us follow at least one man-made teaching within each of our denominations that could prove to be wrong, and scorn all brothers who disagree with us? Remember that no man is right on every issue, be he Calvin, Luther, Zwingli, Wesley, or the leader upon whom your denomination was founded or for whom it is named.

Let's go one step farther. Not only do we break communion with other members of the body of Christ because of denominational distinctives, but we often break fellowship with brothers in our own denomination because of misguided views on secondary separation. Don't misunderstand me. I am a separatist and practice Romans 16:17 and 2 John 7-11. However, separation in these texts is based exclusively on the doctrine of Christ—His deity, virgin birth, blood atonement, bodily resurrection and return—not one's personal standards or rules based on a misinterpretation of these texts.

Scores who hold to these Christological truths have nevertheless been "disfellowshipped" because of their refusal to bow to man-made principles of separation. Further, they are roasted in print and mislabeled as "pseudo-fundamentalists" (fakes) or "neo-evangelicals." The situation is heartbreaking as an ungodly world mocks this brand of Christianity.

Dr. Paul E. Billheimer states, "I believe personally that the main thing hindering the return of the Lord is the disunity of the Body. This is the greatest sin in the Church because it is the real cause of more souls being lost than any other sin. Born-again believers should be united on the basis of a common origin, a common fatherhood, a common parenthood, a common relationship rather than a common opinion on non-essentials. We will never agree theologically. It is my position that if we're born again, we're members of the same family and that is the basis of fellowship, love, and union rather than agreement on the non-essentials."

I, too, was guilty. In my mass, areawide crusades, dating from 1969 to 1980, many good brothers in Christ were barred from participation because I allowed "militant" leaders in numerous cities to establish false standards of separation. Consequently, men who dearly loved God were often banned because they did not bear the same denominational tag. Later, even those within the same group were at one another's throats—each classifying the other as a "pseudo-fundamentalist" or "neo-evangelical" solely on the biased views of a vocal minority. As a result, many good men were deeply hurt. Yet I remained silent.

During the final five years, my spirit grew progressively troubled and many decisions were made. Consequently, I am now able to fulfill the promise I made at the 1977 Sword of the Lord Conference in Detroit. At that time I stated, "I can no longer tolerate the dissension and division occurring among the brethren. It hinders genuine revival and makes a mocking world reject the message of Christ. I will no longer go into areas for future evangelistic campaigns unless there is a new spirit of love and unity among our leaders."

Unfortunately, the love and unity for which my soul cried out did not occur. In fact, the divisiveness became worse. In earlier days, the first 60 of my 253 united crusades to audiences totaling more than 10,000,000 persons were sponsored by scores of solid, evangelical denominations. Before long, however, various exclusions took place, depending on local preferences:

1. All non-Baptistic groups, such as the Nazarenes, Wesleyan Methodists, Free Methodists, Missionary churches, Mennonites, and numerous others—including Dr. A. W. Tozer's great fellowship of Christian and Missionary Alliance churches—were banned. I remember with gratitude the love these brethren in Christ manifested toward me even though they knew they were sponsoring an evangelist who had different denominational tags. D. L. Moody, Billy Sunday, Dr. John R. Rice, and Dr. Bob Jones, Sr. had always included such groups. Thus, a **new** separatist position was instituted.

2. The next move was to eliminate the Grace Brethren fellowship of churches, headquartered at Winona Lake, In-

diana. In addition, depending on geographical location, the Independent Fundamental Churches of America (the group who ordained me) plus other Bible and Community churches were also barred from participation. Extremists would not recognize these brethren because the Baptist label was not above the entrance of their church buildings. Though they were doctrinally sound, as well as Baptistic in practice, they were still banned because they were not considered part of the "Baptist Bride"—a position held by some ultra-denominationalists.

3. Later in my ministry, all Conservative Baptists of America (CBA), along with all Baptist General Conference churches (Swedish), North American German Baptists, Free Will Baptists, and the majority of the remaining Baptist groups were excluded. While they were considered part of the "Baptist Bride," they were shunned on the basis of a "soiled wedding garment." In other words, the "ecclesiastical judges" decided that these brethren had fellowshipped with those whom they had "disfellowshipped," and thus were tainted. At this point, practically everyone had been eliminated.

4. Finally, the "super-separatist society" was reduced to a handful of independents who accused and eliminated one another from participation in united (?) crusades for the souls of men.

Men were now divided over institutions and personalities. Schools such as Asbury College, Biola, Cedarville (GARBC), Calvary Bible College, Dallas Bible College, Dallas Theological Seminary, Detroit Bible College (now William Tyndale College), Florida Bible College, Grace College and Seminary, Grand Rapids Baptist Seminary (GARBC), Grand Rapids School of the Bible (IFCA), John Brown University, Liberty Baptist Seminary, Moody Bible Institute, Tennessee Temple Schools and scores of others were now classified as "moderate fundamentalist institutions who were willing to compromise with neo-evangelicals." (For documentation, see Dr. George Dollar's book, *The History of Fundamentalism.*)

Soon, all pastors who claimed one of these schools as their alma mater were suspect as "pseudo-fundamentalists," "modified fundamentalists" (compromisers) or "neo-evangelicals." On one occasion, I was told by extremist leaders that my appearance at a Moody Founder's Week Conference would result in the cancellation of one or more of my forthcoming city-wide endeavors. Under pressure, I yielded. To this day,

I regret that decision made because religious blackmailers threatened me.

Men were also divided over pantsuits, hair-covered ears and, on one occasion, wire-rimmed glasses. Now, while I believe that every pastor and church has the privilege of setting individual standards, a problem arises when they attempt to force their rules upon others as a basis for fellowship or the sponsorship of crusades. The heartbreaking fact was that those who were so judgmental on these issues involving secondary separation were often lenient concerning sexual promiscuity, smutty jokes, and slander within their personal associations and churches. Hypocrisy abounded, and my heart was crushed. Three of these leaders were arrested for soliciting prostitutes.

I have lived with this heartache long enough. Now it is finished, and my only desire is to love all the family of God and proclaim the message of reconciliation until I go home. How else can I expect to hear my Lord say, "Well done, thou good and faithful servant"?

Prejudice and hatred are never God's will for defenders of the faith. Paul said in 1 Corinthians 13:3, *though I give my body to be burned, and have not charity* [love], *it profiteth me nothing*. Oh, let's get filled with the Spirit! When this happens, love will dominate our beings and we will share that love with all members of the body of Christ, for *the fruit of the*

Spirit is love, joy, peace, longsuffering, gentleness, goodness, faith, meekness, temperance (Galatians 5:22,23).

Because the situation concerning my area-wide crusades became seemingly hopeless, I realized the futility of attempting to reach a world of lost men under these heartbreaking conditions. Thus, I ended this aspect of my ministry, fulfilling my promise made at the Sword of the Lord Conference in 1977. My experience has made me realize how true the following statement, taken from *The Herald of His Coming*, really is:

> Satan is a keen fighter against the body as a whole. The main thing he is driving at on earth is to divide the body. He is adept at divisive tactics. Under one cover or another, he aims to separate one member of the body from another. He knows the tremendous power there is in unity. He knows so well the resistless power against his person when there is united prayer and united action coming from a united body. He will do his utmost to kill that spirit of unity. So anything that divides the body or splits up any group of Christ's followers suits his purpose.

My personal apology to the body of Christ

Beloved brothers in Christ, I reach out to you with open arms of love. If you were ostracized and banned from my crusades, I apologize. I also ask forgiveness for injurying you—a true member of the body of Christ. I promise both my God and you that the rest of my years will be spent proclaiming the message of reconciliation and love for **all** the brotherhood (see 1 Peter 2:17). I cannot do otherwise, for we are all one body in Christ Jesus (1 Corinthians 12:13), and the Holy Spirit adds in verses 25 and 26 that *there should be no schism* [or division] *in the body* because it inflicts agonizing pain upon all of us. Yes, [if] *one member suffer*[s], *all the members suffer with it.*

Brothers and sisters, since I have caused some of this pain in the body of Christ, I once again ask for your forgiveness. I truly love each of you who are members of the family of God and never want to knowingly hurt anyone again.

I conclude by asking all ministers and laymen, "When did you last exemplify the love of Christ to a brother or sister within another denomination—or even within your own if they are of another association or affiliation? If not, why not? Since we are all members of the one Body, are we not "fingers on the same hand," as it were?

What a shame, then, that religious leaders will not allow these fingers—representing various denominational brothers—to touch one another until we reach heaven's golden shores! God forgive all of us. We have been wrong...so drastically wrong...so scripturally wrong!
SHOW LOVE...
to manifest to an unbelieving world that we all **are** one, and that the Father **hath** sent the Son!

Chapter 7

Historic Fundamentalism's Roots

Is love for one another, regardless of denominational affiliation, a scriptural principle? Were our founding fathers right, or were they wrong? You be the judge.

Forty years ago, I met Jesus and was gloriously saved. I shall never forget my newly found joy in the Lord. The experience took place in a small church established by the North American (German) Baptist Conference directly across from my home. As I mentioned in chapter two, in my pagan state, I had often raided this group with rotten tomatoes. Little did I realize that I would one day be led to Jesus Christ by those I had persecuted.

These precious people were Christians first—then Baptists. One thing they taught me was a love for all of God's people. Because of it, I soon shared both my testimony and my talents as an accordionist within numerous denominations. This was an era of interdenominational fellowship, and no one was criticized, stigmatized, or ostracized because of his love for all members of the family of God.

In the '40s, I often heard messages that incorporated the following truth, "When one is a Christian, he can travel anywhere globally and experience intimate fellowship with brethren of like precious faith." How true it was. These were happy days of loving the people of God, regardless of their denominational affiliation.

Fundamentalism's roots

The harmony I experienced and enjoyed was the natural outgrowth of fundamentalism's roots. Separatist denominationalists should sit up and take notice at this point. Apparently they know little about their heritage. Dr. George Dollar, in his book, *A History of Fundamentalism in America*, reports that the who's who of first-generation fundamentalists consisted of leaders identified with the following denominations: Presbyterian, Reformed, Reformed Episcopal, Methodist, Anglican, Baptist, Lutheran, Wesleyan (holiness), and Congregational. By the way, Billy Sunday was a Presbyterian and the revered D. L. Moody, a Congregationalist, as was C. I. Scofield.

What do our roots teach us? Simply that the amalgamated mixture of first-generation fundamentalists included numerous groups composed of Calvinists and Arminians, eternal security advocates and "falling from grace" proponents, pre-millennialists and a-millennialists, sprinklers and immersionists, sacramentalists and the non-sacramentalists who opted for ordinances. Nevertheless, all were rooted in one heart and spirit around the five points of historic fundamentalism:

1. The inspiration and inerrancy of Scripture.
2. The deity of Jesus Christ.
3. The virgin birth of Christ.
4. The substitutionary, atoning work of Christ on the cross.
5. The physical resurrection and the personal, bodily return of Christ to earth.

These five points constituted the basis for withdrawal from liberalism and apostasy, and men from all backgrounds took their stand on these issues—nothing additional.

Today, the waters have become muddied and bloodied by militant leadership. In fact, one may no longer be considered a genuine fundamentalist even though he is so devoted to these five points that he would gladly give his life for his beliefs.

How has all this confusion, bigotry, prejudice, and lovelessness become so pervasive and predominant in a good and God-honoring movement that had such a grand beginning? It happened simply because men whose hearts brimmed with love towards others—men who were basically shy and unassuming—sat idly by and never protested the creation of neo-fundamentalism—a movement that continually added rules, regulations, and resolutions to the five original points at their conferences, convocations, and congresses of fundamentalism.

Dr. Truman Dollar, a prominent leader in the Baptist Bible Fellowship movement of Springfield, Missouri, writes, "The men who contributed to The Fundamentals had widely diverse backgrounds. They were united by their common commitment to the basics (fundamentals) of the Christian faith. In their defense of the faith, they...**refused** to be divided over denominational distinctives or personal biases.

"Since that early coalition, the situation has dramatically changed. There are those within the Fundamentalist movement who want to add their own beliefs and practices to the five fundamentals. Their list continually expands until it eventually excludes everyone who disagrees with any position they represent. The issue is no longer a commitment to the five fundamentals but rather allegiance to what they claim are the 7 fundamentals, the 10 fundamentals, the 20 fundamentals, the 50 fundamentals, and so on."

Dr. Dollar adds, "Who are the real pseudo-fundamentalists? [I prefer the term, "neo-fundamentalists" —JVI] From a historical perspective they are those who have added their personal preferences to the fundamentals and have demanded allegiance to every jot and tittle of THEIR LAW. Within fundamentalism are those who want to saturate the movement with their own brand of additives, [which are] dangerous to the health of the movement and, unrestrained, may produce a cancer that will destroy its life and vitality. Perhaps the time has come to perform major surgery in order to deal with the cancer."

God bless you, Dr. Dollar. You have expressed my sentiments precisely! Since I released my article entitled "That They All May Be One," I have discovered that there are hundreds, yes, even tens of thousands, who are heartsick over the bitterness, prejudice, and name-calling that abounds. These fundamentalists have hearts filled with love and they want change. In such an hour as this, God help us to "walk tall" and protest, whatever the cost. Let's oppose the man-made labels placed upon good and godly men whose only crime is that they will not bow to man as they reject the 7, 10, 20 or 50 points contrary to historic fundamentalism's roots.

Let's also reject the harsh, crude, and intemperate language neo-fundamentalists use in describing others. God commands that we *speak evil of no man* (Titus 3:2), that we *do good unto all men* (Galatians 6:10), that our *speech be alway*[s] *with grace* (Colossians 4:6), and that *all* [our] *things be done with* [love] (1 Corinthians 16:14).

There was a period of time in my life when I thought God was pleased with my abusive verbal assaults on other men and movements. Then the Holy Spirit began to do a deep work within my being, convicting me of my ungraciousness. I now know that *the servant of the Lord must not strive; but be gentle unto all men* (2 Timothy 2:24). If God could do this work of grace in my heart, I'm certain He can do it for others.

In the flesh, this is an impossibility. However, through the infilling of the Holy Spirit, it becomes a reality. Then *love, joy, peace, long-suffering, gentleness, goodness, faith, meekness* [and],*temperance* (Galatians 5:22,23) will become evident. When the Spirit controls men and movements, we will *be kindly affectioned one to another* (Romans 12:10) and will *do good unto all men, especially unto them who are of the household of faith* (Galatians 6:10). Then we will *increase and abound in love one toward another* (1 Thessalonians 3:12) and overlook the faults of others as love covers a multitude of sins (see 1 Peter 4:8)—and perhaps a few mistakes as well. Then love will no longer be thought of as a sentimental sickness inherent in compromisers, but a healthy wholesomeness within Spirit-controlled brethren.

Fundamentalism's silent majority— men of love and compassion

I have read many fundamentalist publications and heard numerous innuendoes concerning my new position. One stated that I was attempting to unite cultists and evangelicals!

None of the statements and accusations were true. Some of my friends encouraged me to retaliate. I did not. I rest upon the promise of my heavenly Father who said, *Be still, and know that I am God* (Psalm 46:10). Time heals all wounds. I will wait.

At this point, may I simply say that I am a historic fundamentalist who would lay down his life for the five foundational points because they center around my wonderful Lord and the Book that is so precious to me. As such, I will love all blood-bought members of God's family because this is a scriptural principle preached and practiced by historic fundamentalists. I stand where the late Dr. John R. Rice stood when he so often stated with great dogmatism in *The Sword of The Lord...I am a companion of all them that fear thee* (Psalm 119:63).

Rexella and I have vowed before the Lord that LOVE FOR ALL THE FAMILY OF GOD will be our new position until Christ calls us home. We agreed that, if this conviction cost us the loss of numerous supporters, or even the dissolution of our national television ministry, we would gladly pay the price. In fact, we prepared the following letter for the great number we thought would cancel their prayer and financial support.

Dear Brother:

With respect to your concern about the direction I am taking, may I immediately state that the only change is that the sweet Spirit of the Lord has broadened my convictions to practice all of God's Word, including John 13:35 and 1 John 4:7,8,12,20.

In my article entitled, "That They All May Be One," I said, "I promise God and all members of His family that the remainder of my life will be spent proclaiming the message of reconciliation and love for ALL the brotherhood" (see 1 Peter 2:17). I meant this. I will live and die for this biblical principle called love.

If my position causes you to withdraw your church's prayer and financial support, that must be your decision before God. Even if all men follow your example and I become financially unable to continue my ministry, I will know that I have obeyed God and His commandment to love one another—and nothing else matters.

Sincerely in Christ,
Jack Van Impe

Instead of having to use this letter often, hundreds wrote to say, "Brother Van Impe, we, too, are fundamentalists standing where you do on this matter of love. We also are grieved by the rampant divisiveness within our movement, and thank God for the breath of fresh air the Spirit of God is sending our way through your new position of love."

Fundamentalism's marching orders

Is love for one another, regardless of denominational affiliation, a scriptural principle? Were our founding fathers right, or were they wrong? You be the judge.

ORDER #1: Every born-again believer is a member of the body of Christ.

In Christ's great priestly prayer, recorded in John 17:11,21-23, He prayed for unity four times. Dr. Lewis Sperry Chafer says, "With all these requests in view, it must be conceded that few, if any, truths are so emphasized in the Word of God as the Unity of the believers. Now this prayer began to be answered on the Day of Pentecost when those then saved were fused into one body. The prayer has also been answered continuously as all those at the moment of believing were added to Christ's body by the operation of the Holy Spirit (see 1 Corinthians 12:13). This marvelous unity between believers then becomes the logical ground for all Christian action [namely, love —JVI] one toward another."

79

Presently, it is the duty of every Christian to keep the unity the Holy Spirit has already begun and continued for 20 centuries (see Ephesians 4:1-3). This is God's commandment, and no set of resolutions by any group can alter God's marching orders.

ORDER #2: Every born-again believer is a member of the family of God.

Ephesians 3:15 speaks of the family as being *in heaven and* [upon] *earth.* What does the verse mean? Those who have died in Jesus are already present in glory, *absent from the body...present with the Lord* (2 Corinthians 5:8). Hence, all family members—spanning 2,000 years of Christendom—now in heaven await the homecoming of family members still upon earth. Now get it, this is important: These believers in heaven and upon earth got there by being saved in thousands of denominations in which they were members during their lifetime. Since there is no way one can get rid of his spiritual relatives in heaven or upon earth (the saved from thousands of denominations covering 20 centuries), let's LOVE THEM—especially the ones still breathing!

ORDER #3: Every born-again believer is a son or daughter of God.

As many as received him, to them gave he power to become the sons of God (John 1:12).

Since none of us has the right to eliminate or ignore our brothers or sisters within the family, I suggest that we begin to *LOVE THE BROTHERHOOD* (1 Peter 2:17).

ORDER #4: Every born-again believer is the Lord's by adoption (Ephesians 1:5).

Scriptural adoption means that the new "babe in Christ" is placed into the family as an adult son or daughter, with all the rights and privileges of one who has reached legal age (21, in America). These rights make every child an heir of God and *joint-heirs with* [Jesus] *Christ* (Romans 8:17).

ORDER #5: Every born-again believer has been cleansed by the blood of Jesus (1 John 1:7).

And *what God hath cleansed, that call not thou common* [or unclean] (Acts 11:9).

ORDER #6: Every born-again believer has been forgiven.

In [Christ] *we have redemption through his blood, the forgiveness of sins, according to the riches of his grace* (Ephesians 1:7).

ORDER #7: Every born-again believer has been redeemed or bought back from the slave market of sin and set free through the precious blood of Jesus (1 Peter 1:19).

81

This includes every child of God saved in every gospel-preaching denomination.

ORDER # 8: Every born-again believer has been reconciled (2 Corinthians 5:19,20).

This means that every brother in Christ is eternally at peace with God. Since God has been so gracious to us, we, in turn, should practice Hebrews 12:14 which commands us to *follow peace with all men, and holiness, without which no man shall see the Lord.*

ORDER #9: Every born again believer has been regenerated (Titus 3:5), meaning that life and the divine nature have been imparted to him (2 Peter 1:4).

This includes every child of God who ever got it, gets it, or ever will get it in the years ahead as Jesus tarries. Sad, is it not, that many Christians are forbidden to fellowship with believers who have God's own nature? No wonder new converts are confused.

ORDER #10: Every born-again believer has been *made nigh* or close to God by the blood of Jesus (Ephesians 2:13).

No one is any closer to God than another on the basis of denominational merit. Instead, this nearness is based on a blood relationship—that of the Lamb of God. Thank God this is so, for there are presently 20,780 distinct Christian denominations now locatable in Christian atlases internationally—and a great percentage of them uplift Jesus.

ORDER #11: Every born-again believer has been *accepted in the beloved* [Jesus] (Ephesians 1:6).

Our acceptance is on the basis that we have become *the righteousness of God in him* [Christ] (2 Corinthians 5:21). This includes all "relatives" found in all Bible-believing churches. Don't forget it. If every child of God is *accepted in the beloved*, perhaps we should show a little more kindness to all of our relatives in Christ Jesus.

ORDER #12: Every born-again believer is a citizen of heaven.

Philippians 3:20 declares, *For our conversation* [citizenship] *is in heaven.* Because of it, we *are no more strangers and foreigners, but fellow-citizens with the saints, and of the household of God* (Ephesians 2:19). This citizenship is bestowed upon red, yellow, black, and white, completed Jews and Gentiles, Calvinists and Arminians, pre-Tribulationists and post-Tribulationists, pre-millennialists and a-millennialists! Anyone who has put his faith and trust in Christ has a passport for heaven, and no militant group passing resolutions making good men "pseudo-fundamentalists" or "neo-evangelicals" can change that.

ORDER #13: Every born-again believer has been "justified" or declared absolutely righteous—just as if he had never sinned.

This is because of the merits of the shed blood of Jesus (see Romans 5:9). If this be true—and it is—I find it ridiculous that most of us are forbidden fellowship with other brothers and sisters of like precious faith who have been declared absolutely righteous in Jesus. What bigots we denominationalists and separatists often are.

ORDER #14: Every born-again believer is a member of the *royal priesthood* (1 Peter 2:9).

Even this status symbol is ignored in our separatist "caste system."

ORDER #15: Every born-again believer (you Calvinists will love this) has been:
  A. Chosen in Him before the foundation of the world (Ephesians 1:4).
  B. Elected (Romans 8:33).
  C. Called with an holy calling (2 Timothy 1:9; Hebrews 1:14).
  D. Drawn by the Father (John 6:44).
  E. Given to Christ by the Father (John 6:37).

F. Predestined to be conformed to the image of his Son (Romans 8:29).

Imagine! The omniscient, all-knowing God planned in centuries past to save His children in thousands of denominations, spanning a period of approximately 2,000 years. He placed the first convert into the "body" of Christ at Pentecost, and will continue the process until the final member completes the one body. Just think—if the Father had not bungled the job (according to some denominationalists), the situation might have been so different. If He had planned to save all His chosen in one group, we would not have had to make as many resolutions against others.

Well, since the all-wise God did it His way, and since this includes every saved person in Baptist, Presbyterian, Methodist, Episcopalian, Lutheran, Reformed, Wesleyan, Free Methodist, Pilgrim Holiness, Nazarene, and Pentecostal churches—recognize that God did it and accept His eternal plan. Then decide to love and accept all those HE included. He made no mistakes. But you do, when you reject His foreordained plan.

ORDER #16: Every born-again believer is already seated *in heavenly places in Christ Jesus* (Ephesians 2:6).

Theologically and biblically, this is acceptable. However, let's not practice this truth until we get there. Presently, let's not even sit with them in a restaurant—we might be suspected of compromise!

Have I made the scriptural position clear? I am not talking about anyone's forfeiting his denominational distinctives or giving up his doctrinal position. However, I **am** saying that because of our unity as members of the "one body," we must love one another.

Someone may be asking, "What about the verses that command us to 'avoid them' 'come out from among them,' 'judge them,' 'reprove them,' 'mark them,' 'identify them,' 'withdraw from them,' 'turn away from them,' 'reject them,' 'keep not company with them' and 'note them?'" In the next chapter, I will deal with the meaning of the term "them."

In conclusion, if I have gotten through to your mind and heart via these tremendous scriptural truths, would you pray and ask forgiveness for your hardness of heart and prejudices? I came to this point and asked forgiveness of both God and men. My article entitled, "That They All May Be One," reprinted in chapter six, tells of my seven-year battle with the truths presented in this article. The Scriptures were plain, and I had to obey. Will you?

Don't let carnal leaders misguide you. Remember, *and now abideth faith, hope, charity* [love], *these three; but the greatest of these is charity* [love](1 Corinthians 13:13). So, *let brotherly love continue* (Hebrews 13:1).

In addition to the 16 marching orders contained in the message itself, I include the following commands for your further consideration and blessing.

17. EVERY BORN-AGAIN BELIEVER is *the salt of the earth* (Matthew 5:13).
18. EVERY BORN-AGAIN BELIEVER is *the light of the world* (Matthew 5:14).
19. EVERY BORN-AGAIN BELIEVER possesses *everlasting life* (John 3:36).
20. EVERY BORN-AGAIN BELIEVER is one of God's sheep (John 10:27).
21. EVERY BORN-AGAIN BELIEVER is a saint (Romans 1:7).
22. EVERY BORN-AGAIN BELIEVER has been *baptized into Jesus Christ* (Romans 6:3-5).
23. EVERY BORN-AGAIN BELIEVER is free from condemnation (Romans 8:1).
24. EVERY BORN-AGAIN BELIEVER is inseparable *from the love of God* (Romans 8:38,39).
25. EVERY BORN-AGAIN BELIEVER is *sanctified* (1 Corinthians 1:2).
26. EVERY BORN-AGAIN BELIEVER is a partaker of God's grace (1 Corinthians 1:4).

27. EVERY BORN-AGAIN BELIEVER is confirmed to the end (1 Corinthians 1:8).
28. EVERY BORN-AGAIN BELIEVER is *called* [into] *the fellowship of his Son* (1 Corinthians 1:9).
29. EVERY BORN-AGAIN BELIEVER is a part of *God's building* (1 Corinthians 3:9).
30. EVERY BORN-AGAIN BELIEVER is the temple of God (1 Corinthians 3:16).
31. EVERY BORN-AGAIN BELIEVER is *the temple of* the Holy Spirit (1 Corinthians 6:19).
32. EVERY BORN-AGAIN BELIEVER drinks *the same spiritual drink* (1 Corinthians 10:4).
33. EVERY BORN-AGAIN BELIEVER partakes of one bread (1 Corinthians 10:17).
34. EVERY BORN-AGAIN BELIEVER is gifted (1 Corinthians 12:7).
35. EVERY BORN-AGAIN BELIEVER is sealed (2 Corinthians 1:22).
36. EVERY BORN-AGAIN BELIEVER is a *sweet savour of Christ* (2 Corinthians 2:15).
37. EVERY BORN-AGAIN BELIEVER has a new house or bodily covering awaiting him in heaven (2 Corinthians 5:1).
38. EVERY BORN-AGAIN BELIEVER is a new creation (2 Corinthians 5:17).
39. EVERY BORN-AGAIN BELIEVER is

an ambassador for Christ (2 Corinthians 5:20).

40. EVERY BORN-AGAIN BELIEVER is one of God's people (2 Corinthians 6:16).

41. EVERY BORN-AGAIN BELIEVER is a child of Abraham, spiritually (Galatians 3:7).

42. EVERY BORN-AGAIN BELIEVER has been *redeemed from the curse of the law* (Galatians 3:13).

43. EVERY BORN-AGAIN BELIEVER is Christ's purchased possession (Ephesians 1:13,14).

44. EVERY BORN-AGAIN BELIEVER is saved by grace (Ephesians 2:8,9).

45. EVERY BORN-AGAIN BELIEVER is God's workmanship (Ephesians 2:10).

46. EVERY BORN-AGAIN BELIEVER is a child of light (Ephesians 5:8).

47. EVERY BORN-AGAIN BELIEVER has been delivered from darkness (Colossians 1:13).

48. EVERY BORN-AGAIN BELIEVER has an *eternal inheritance* (Hebrews 9:15).

49. EVERY BORN-AGAIN BELIEVER is already perfected in Christ (Hebrews 10:14).

50. EVERY BORN-AGAIN BELIEVER is a king (Revelation 5:10).

After studying this tremendous additional listing as to what every child of God is or shall be, don't you agree it is sad that we are often asked to reject brothers and sisters in whom God has performed such mighty works?

Chapter 8

Neo-Fundamentalism's Errant Interpretation of the Inerrant Word

Two misinterpreted biblical texts have been used to create the greatest mistrust of brothers in the history of Christendom.

The twentieth century began with a tumultuous conservative uproar over the infiltration of numerous denominations by liberalism. The severity of the situation demanded immediate action. Heretical teachings were captivating and corrupting entire churches, schools, and related organizations within multiplied denominations. Therefore, a coalition of interdenominational brethren, following a number of conferences, united around the five fundamentals of the faith. They were:
1. The inspiration and inerrancy of Scripture.
2. The deity of Jesus Christ.
3. The virgin birth of Christ.
4. The substitutionary, atoning work of Christ on the cross.

5. The physical resurrection and the personal, bodily return of Christ to the earth.

The adherents to these five fundamental truths were naturally labeled "fundamentalists." Those opposing them were called "liberals."

The men joining together around these five points (commonly called "the doctrine of Christ") were from varied and diversified religious backgrounds. Thus, this amalgamation of "first generation fundamentalists" included Presbyterians, Baptists, Reformers, Reformed Episcopalians, Lutherans, Methodists, Anglicans, Congregationalists, and Wesleyan Holiness brothers. The astounding thing about the members of this interdenominational movement was their love for one another. All secondary differences concerning personal preferences and denominational distinctives were laid aside. Their only burden and goal was to glorify the Lord Jesus Christ. They were "warriors" in a battle against liberalism and they knew who the *enemies of the cross of Christ* (Philippians 3:18) were.

Historians inform us that all conferences leading up to the formation of this glorious and biblically oriented movement were non-sectarian. Denominational positions were never discussed or debated. Wouldn't it be spiritually stimulating to turn back history's clock a mere eighty years and re-experience the overwhelming love brothers in Christ had for one another under the banner of interdenominational funda-mentalism? Wouldn't it be glorious to fellow-ship with others of like precious faith without being suspected of committing a traitorous act of compromise?

Today, suspicion abounds and condemna-tory pronouncements increase against good men and organizations simply because man-made in-novations, standards, and rules have become the tests of fellowship. The "doctrine of Christ" alone is no longer the standard. Instead, man's misinterpretations of Scripture are. May God allow us to see the situation and deal with such destructive additives before it is too late. The cancer is growing, and it may soon destroy our movement. To understand the situation perfect-ly, let's look at fundamentalism in detail.

Fundamentalism's separatist stance

Dr. Ed Dobson, editor of *The Fundamental-ist Journal*, presents us with a brief historical sketch of the movement. He states, "Fundamen-talism's war in the '20s was a vibrant demon-stration of the church's responsibility to defend the faith from doctrinal heresy. The clear teach-ing of Scripture mandated a confrontation with heresy and separation from it (see 1 John 4:1-3; 2 Peter 2:1; Romans 16:17,18; 2 John 10,11). The war concluded with Fundamentalists with-drawing from the mainline denominations and forming their own fellowships, schools, and organizations. Truth had been defended and purity maintained. However, the unity that these early Fundamentalists demonstrated was quickly dissipated as each group set about the task of rebuilding and recuperating from the aftermath of the bloody conflict.

"Over fifty years have elapsed since that controversy. We have continued to defend the truth and have remained loyal recipients of our religious heritage. However, we are not without our extremes and excuses. Like our forefathers, we have a fallible tendency to overreact. In our sincere desire to maintain purity, we sometimes go beyond the guidelines of Scripture and reason. There are these polemic Fundamentalists who have added their own personal convictions to the historic list of fundamentals. They insist on conformity to all THEIR VIEWS and failure to do so means immediate examination by their group. Anyone outside their fold [and there are numerous folds, each with its own standards — JVI] is considered suspect. Their desire for internal purity leaves them critical of everyone else who claims the same Saviour. It is one thing to go to war against heresy. It is another thing to go to war against a Christian brother."

I wholeheartedly agree with our founding fathers in their separatist stance. Liberal theologians denying the deity of Christ, His virgin birth, the substitutionary atoning work of Christ upon the cross, the physical resurrection and the personal, bodily return of the Lord Jesus Christ are definitely apostates. Webster's dictionary defines an *apostate* as "one who has departed or defected from the faith." Apostates are also described in 1 John 2:19, *They went out from us, but they were not of us; for if they had been of us, they would no doubt have continued with us: but they went out, that they might be made manifest that they were not all of us.* In defecting and turning away from the doctrine of Christ, they actually renounced the faith, for 1 John 2:23 declares, *Whosoever denieth the Son, the same hath not the Father: (but) he that acknowledgeth the Son hath the Father also.* Thus, their departure made them false prophets and teachers to be avoided. John warns, *Beloved, believe not every spirit* [teacher], *but try* [test] *the spirits* [teachers]*whether they are of God: because many false prophets are gone out into the world. Hereby know ye the Spirit of God: Every spirit* [teacher] *that confesseth that Jesus Christ* [God] *is come in the flesh is of God: and every spirit* [teacher] *that confesseth not that Jesus Christ is come in the flesh is not of God: and this is that spirit of antichrist, whereof ye have heard that it should come; and even now already is it in the world* (1 John 4:1-3).

Now since apostates were and are antichrists, and because two cannot walk together unless they be agreed (see Amos 3:3), there was only one course of action possible for fundamental-

95

ism's founding fathers—total severance and separation from such outrageous unbelief. This position was based upon such scriptural texts as 2 Corinthians 6:14-18:

Be ye not unequally yoked together with unbelievers: for what fellowship hath righteousness with unrighteousness? and what communion hath light with darkness? And what concord hath Christ with Belial? or what part hath he that believeth with an infidel? And what agreement hath the temple of God with idols? for ye are the temple of the living God; as God hath said, I will dwell in them, and walk in them; and I will be their God, and they shall be my people. Wherefore come out from among them, and be ye separate, saith the Lord, and touch not the unclean thing; and I will receive you, and will be a Father unto you, and ye shall be my sons and daughters, saith the Lord Almighty.

We see, then, that our separatist stance began as a biblically oriented position against apostasy. We severed religious connections with those who denied the five-point teaching concerning Christ and the inerrant Bible. This was a good and just platform for fundamentalism since Christ alone was our standard, our rallying point. What one thinks about Christ separates the wheat from the tares, the just from the unjust, the genuine from the false, and the apostates from the children of God.

This is the position I embraced as a God-given conviction years ago. I have not changed. The rules have changed, but I have not. In fact, I am still so committed to Christ and His Word, and so opposed to apostasy, that I delivered the following message via national television:

What does the Bible have to say about apostasy? I realize that I shall be called an apostle of discord, a cultist, a hyper-fundamentalist and an extremist but I couldn't care less. I stand with the great Apostle Paul who said in Galatians 1:10, *If I yet pleased men, I should not be the servant of Christ.*

Now there are two ways to say it. One is to use such a profound vocabulary that all will be astounded at my intelligence but probably never get the message. The other is to say it with all the simplicity that God meant for it to be given so that everyone gets the plain truth. For instance, I can say, "In promulgating your esoteric cogitations or articulating your superficial sentimentalities and amicable, philosophical or psychological observations, beware of platitudinous ponderosity." Or, in simpler terms, "Keep your talking simple and to the point." Let me do just that.

First of all, the Bible teaches that apostates will arise within the Christian church. *For I know this, that after my departing shall grievous wolves enter in among you, not sparing the flock* (Acts 20:29).

But there were false prophets also among the people, even as there shall be [future tense] *false teachers among you, who privily* [or secretly] *shall bring in damnable heresies, even denying the Lord that bought them, and bring upon themselves swift destruction* (2 Peter 2:1).

For there are certain men crept in unawares, who were before of old ordained to this condemnation, ungodly men, turning the grace of our God into lasciviousness, and denying the only Lord God, and our Lord Jesus Christ (Jude:4).

Notice carefully—they creep in very secretly, quietly, and slowly and, once they are in, they take over and deny the Lord Jesus Christ. This has to do, you see, with the fundamentals of the doctrine of Christ: His deity (1 Timothy 3:16), His virgin birth (Matthew 1:23), His substitutionary blood atonement (1 Corinthians 15:3; Ephesians 1:7), His bodily resurrection (Romans 4:25; 10:9,10) and His bodily return

(1 Thessalonians 4:16,17; Matthew 24:44).

Second, the Bible describes the great damage apostates do. They spare not *the flock* [God's people] (Acts 20:29). They *cause divisions and offences...*[and] *deceive the hearts of the simple* (Romans 16:17,18). They *speak lies in hypocrisy* (1 Timothy 4:2). They *consent not to wholesome words, even the words of our Lord Jesus Christ* (1 Timothy 6:3). They *overthrow the faith of some* (2 Timothy 2:18). Oh, how true and how sad! They *bring in damnable heresies, even denying the Lord* (2 Peter 2:1). *They are not afraid to speak evil of dignities...*[they] *speak evil of the things that they understand not...*[They have] *eyes full of adultery, and that cannot cease from sin; beguiling unstable souls...*[They] *have forsaken the right way, and...they speak great swelling words of vanity,* or use a great vocabulary to draw men to themselves (2 Peter 2:10,12,14,15,18). They *confess not that Jesus Christ is come in the flesh* (2 John 7). They abide not in the doctrine of God. They turn *the grace of our God into lasciviousness, and* [deny] *the only...Lord Jesus Christ* (Jude 4).

Notice how often the Bible states that they deny Jesus Christ. This is what apostasy is all about. Anyone who says, "I will not accept the doctrine of the virgin birth, His deity, His blood atonement, His bodily resurrection, and His second coming" is an apostate, even if he has a collar or a doctorate in religion. Flee from him!

Third, consider the names and titles God gives to apostates. God? Yes, God! Why do I say this? Because 2 Timothy 3:16 says, *All scripture is given by inspiration of God.* So, in Acts 20:29, God calls apostates *grievous wolves.* In 2 Corinthians 6:14, God calls apostates *unbelievers.* In 2 Corinthians 11:13, God calls apostates *false apostles* and *deceitful workers.* In Philippians 3:18, God calls apostates *the enemies of the cross of Christ.*

In 1 Timothy 6:5, God calls apostates *men of corrupt minds, and destitute of the truth.* In 2 Timothy 2:20, God calls apostates *vessels of...dishonour.* In 2 Peter 2:1, God calls apostates *false teachers.* In 2 Peter 2:12, God calls apostates *natural brute beasts.* God said it, I didn't. Don't get mad at me. He wrote it, I only quote it. In 2 Peter 2:19, God calls apostates *servants of corruption.* Now here is the one I want you to get. In 1 John 2:18, God calls apostates *antichrists.*

Fourth, and finally, consider God's commands to desert these apostates.

Romans 16:17, 2 Corinthians 6:14-18, and 2 John 7-11. Thus it is obvious that God demands separation from apostates, but not from godly brothers.

If this be so—and it is—what is the root cause of all the present confusion within fundamentalism? Is all this castigation and vilification of men and movements biblically based? In search of the answer, I delved into a major study of every separatist text, studying the writings of 65 prominent theologians. Their conclusions are tremendously interesting in our era of confusion. Don't swallow every word—hook, line, and sinker—heard at congresses and conferences on fundamentalism. In some instances, the interpretations are grossly twisted. Let's analyze the separatist texts as they appear in their New Testament settings.

Fundamentalism's position on apostates

1. AVOID THEM. *Now I beseech you, brethren, mark them which cause divisions and of-*

fences contrary to the doctrine which ye have learned; and AVOID THEM (Romans 16:17).

The consensus of many theologians is that the culprits to be avoided in this portion of God's Word are "Antinomian Libertines," purveyors and perpetrators of error about licentious and lewd living. This crowd lived for the complete gratification of every fleshly lust in existence and condoned such lifestyles under the guise of Christian liberty. They said, "If the fulfillment of our sexual and bodily appetites portrays God as a merciful being, then it is for His glory. For where sin abounds, grace does much more abound" (see Romans 5:20). This is the same group of lust-ridden leeches described as *enemies of the cross of Christ* in Philippians 3:18,19. The doctrine over which they were causing divisions and offences was "liberty" versus "holiness." Because of their abominable practices and their proclamation and promotion of this lifestyle, they were to be avoided. Dr. H. A. Ironside says, "The evil doers here referred to are not Christian teachers. They are ungodly men. In Philippians 3:18, we have the identical wretched division markers." Drs. Richard De-Haan, W. R. Newell, Charles Ellicott, Albert Barnes, and Adam Clarke subscribe to the above interpretation.

2. COME OUT FROM AMONG THEM. *Be*

ye not unequally yoked together with unbelievers: for what fellowship hath righteousness with unrighteousness? and what communion hath light with darkness? And what concord hath Christ with Belial? or what part hath he that believeth with an infidel? And what agreement hath the temple of God with idols? for ye are the temple of the living God; as God hath said, I will dwell in them; and walk in them; and I will be their God, and they shall be my people. Wherefore come out from among them, and be ye separate, saith the Lord, and touch not the unclean thing; and I will receive you, and will be a Father unto you, and ye shall be my sons and daughters, saith the Lord Almighty (2 Corinthians 6:14-18).

This text is self-explanatory. Believers are not to be yoked together with unbelievers, especially in religious endeavors. Five reasons are listed as to why such a union becomes impossible. Separation, then, is not only logical but compulsory. Should there be a question as to who the unbelievers are, they are not only atheists denying the existence of God but also religious apostates who deny the doctrine of Christ. Genuine believers wholeheartedly accept 1 John 5:1 which states, *Whosoever believeth that Jesus is the Christ is born of God.* When this truth is denied within a group, one is to come out from among them.

3. JUDGE THEM. *But though we, or an angel from heaven, preach any other gospel unto you than that which we have preached unto you, let him be accursed* (Galatians 1:8).

The judged in this portion of Scripture are legalistic teachers. In Paul's day, they attempted to bring God's children under bondage as they commanded them to *observe days, and months, and times, and years* (Galatians 4:10). Since they were mutilating the message of "grace" proclaimed by Paul, the Apostle of Grace, they were to be shunned and accursed.

Dr. W. A. Criswell states, "The churches founded by the Apostle are in danger of apostascizing, turning aside and back to the beggarly elements of the law" (see Galatians 4:9,10). This is the viewpoint held by Drs. Ramsey, Luther, Ironside, Black, and Ellicott.

4. REPROVE THEM. *And have no fellowship with the unfruitful works of darkness, but rather REPROVE THEM* (Ephesians 5:11).

The *unfruitful works of darkness* with which believers are not to *fellowship* are undeniably *the children of disobedience* of verse 6. The contextual setting makes it abundantly clear that these evil doers are not brothers in Christ, as verses 3-8,11,12 plainly, loudly, and clearly prove. Let's investigate. *But fornication, and all uncleanness, or covetousness, let it not be once named among you, as becometh saints; neither filthiness, nor foolish talking, nor jesting* [telling dirty jokes], *which are not convenient: but rather giving of thanks. For this ye know, that no whoremonger, nor unclean person, nor covetous man, who is an idolater, hath any inheritance in the kingdom of Christ and of God. Let no man deceive you with vain words: for because of these things cometh the wrath of God upon the children of disobedience. Be not ye therefore partakers with them. For ye were sometimes darkness, but now are ye light in the Lord: walk as children of light: and have no fellowship with the unfruitful works of darkness* [the sins and sinners described in the foregoing], *but rather REPROVE THEM. For it is a shame even to speak of those things which are done of them in secret.*

It is obvious that this crowd had an insatiable appetite for lustful pursuits. Concerning them, Paul tells us in chapter 4, verse 19, [They] *being past feeling* [as far as their consciences are concerned] *have given themselves over unto lasciviousness, to work all uncleanness with greediness.* Isn't it shocking that the individuals to be REPROVED are not brethren who fellowship with brethren who fellowship with brethren who fellowshipped with a compromiser, but rather those who practice and promote promiscuity in thought, word, or deed? How wrong in God's sight to jestfully make sport of acts such as adultery or homosexuality, sinful pursuits outside the bonds of holy matrimony. Brethren, we are to break fellowship with all practitioners of lust, as well as covetous personalities whose lives exemplify a "greedy graspingness" for material things and money.

Are such resolutions passed and practiced at our fundamentalist convocations? Are leaders censured for such wickedness? If not, why not? Recently, I saw a "separatist" praised in print for staunchly defending the faith. This man and others in the movement are known to have a repertoire of "smutty jokes" that would make a pirate blush. Why then are such men praised while brothers who fellowship with brothers of different denominations are condemned? It is because men obey the commands that suit them and disregard the ones that convict them.

What are we to do with religious leaders who love wine, women, and song, who live for the flesh, tell obscene jokes, and greedily grasp for monetary gain? God says, *Have no fellowship with the unfruitful works of darkness*. Oh, but the crowd to be shunned in Ephesians 5:11 are sinners. Yes, but *as* [a man] *thinketh in his heart, so is he* (Proverbs 23:7), and *out of the abundance of the heart the mouth speaketh* (Matthew 12:34). Could this be why Matthew 7:22 has religious leaders saying at Judgment Day, *Lord, Lord, have we not prophesied in thy name?*

106

and in thy name have cast out devils? and in thy name done many wonderful works? Verse 23 adds, *And then will I profess unto them, I never knew you: depart from me, ye that work iniquity.*

The greatest tragedy of the present situation within fundamentalism is that those who often shout the loudest about "separation" and brand good and godly men as pseudo-fundamentalists and new evangelicals are often guilty of the sins mentioned in Ephesians 5:3-12 and 1 Corinthians 5:11.

5. MARK THEM. *Brethren, be followers together of me, and mark them which walk so as ye have us for an ensample* [example]. *(For many walk, of whom I have told you often, and now tell you even weeping, that they are the enemies of the cross of Christ)* (Philippians 3:17,18).

Our theologians again agree totally that this is the same crowd mentioned in Romans 16:17— Antinomian libertines who lived for fleshly pleasure.

Dr. Kenneth Wuest says, "The enemies in this text are professing Christian Greeks of Epicurean tendencies. They taught that the satisfaction of the physical appetites were the highest aim of man." Dr. J. B. Lightfoot states, "The persons here denounced are the Antinomian reactionists. The view is borne out in the parallel expression of Romans 16:17-19. They degraded the true doctrine of liberty so as to minister to their profligate and worldly living. These Antinomians refused to conform to the cross by living a life of self indulgence."

Dr. H. A. Ironside adds, "This crowd lived for self indulgence." Interesting, isn't it, that we now have three texts—Romans 16:17, Ephesians 5:11, and Philippians 3:17-19—that command us to "avoid," "reprove," and "mark" those who live for the flesh. Perhaps we need to rethink our position. If we separatists practiced the three texts mentioned above in their entirety, perhaps our religious superiority and cockiness against others might come to a screeching halt. At least it would make us think twice before censuring others.

6. IDENTIFY THEM. First Timothy 1:20, 2 Timothy 1:15; 4:14.

These texts expose Alexander and Hymenaeus as blasphemers, and Phygellus and Hermogenes as defectors. Thus they are identified as apostates, for 1 John 2:19 states, *They went out* [or turned away]...*that they might be made manifest that they were not all of us.* Wycliff says, "Alexander opposed the apostolic teaching. Hymenaeus was a heretic, teaching that the resurrection was past already."

Drs. M. R. DeHann, Ironside, Barnes, and numerous others identify these men as apostates. Let's begin identifying and exposing the right crowd.

7. WITHDRAW FROM THEM. *If any man teach otherwise, and consent not to wholesome words, even the words of our Lord Jesus Christ, and to the doctrine which is according to godliness; He is proud, knowing nothing, but doting about questions and strifes of words, whereof cometh envy, strife, railings, evil surmisings, perverse disputings of men of corrupt minds, and destitute of the truth, supposing that gain is godliness: from such withdraw thyself* (1 Timothy 6:3-5).

The late Dr. Paul R. Jackson, former head of the General Association of Regular Baptist Churches, in his booklet, *The Position, Attitudes and Objective of Biblical Separation*, states, "False doctrine is another basis of separation." I totally agree. Believers are to withdraw from those who propagate doctrinal error.

What specific error existed during Timothy's era that made such a command necessary? Let's investigate. At this point in history, servants were purchased and possessed, even by believers. At times, servants professing to know Christ belittled their Christian masters. Their remarks were so ungracious that sinners blasphemed God as they watched such relationships. They said, "If employees and employers who claim to be saved experience such friction among themselves, don't tell us that Christ meets every need." What caused this problem? The example of Jesus, as found in His teachings, was being ignored. He said, *I am among you as he that serveth* (Luke 22:27), and *whosoever will be chief among you, let him be your servant: even as the Son of Man came not to be ministered unto, but to minister, and to give his life a ransom for many* (Matthew 20:27,28).

Since these were undoubtedly the wholesome words of Christ mentioned by Paul in 1 Timothy 6:3-5, those who rejected His teachings were labeled "arrogant ignoramuses." They spent all their time bickering over the interpretation of the words instead of abiding by them. The results of such nonsensical prattling led to jealousy, strife, railings, evil surmising (suspicious, hidden thoughts about others), and perverse disputings (or protracted wranglings and battles) among them. Paul tells us why they reacted as they did. They were *men of corrupt minds, and destitute of the truth* (verse 5). Or more simply, "They were corrupted in mind and had put away the truth they once possessed." Thus they became defectors or apostates according to 1 John 2:19, and withdrawal from them was necessary.

Drs. Clarke, Hinson, Ellicott, and Vincent concur.

8. TURN AWAY FROM THEM. *Having a*

110

form of godliness, but denying the power thereof: from such turn away (2 Timothy 3:5).

These are professors of religion but not possessors of Christ. Jesus described them in Mark 7:6 saying, *Well hath Esaias prophesied of you hypocrites, as it is written, This people honoureth me with their lips, but their heart is far from me.* Dr. Albert Barnes says, "This group opposed the real power of religion, not allowing it to exert any influence in their lives. They lived as if they had no religion." Dr. Adam Clarke adds, "These mentioned in the text have all their religion in their creed, confession of faith and catechism but are destitute of the life of God in their souls."

Since their lives made a mockery of the faith they professed, genuine believers were to "turn away" from such counterfeits.

9.   REBUKE THEM. *For there are many unruly and vain talkers and deceivers, specially they of the circumcision: whose mouths must be stopped, who subvert whole houses, teaching things which they ought not, for filthy lucre's sake. One of themselves, even a prophet of their own, said, The Cretians are alway liars, evil beasts, slow bellies. This witness is true. Wherefore rebuke them sharply, that they may be sound in the faith* (Titus 1:10-13).

The unruly talkers and deceivers described

111

in the text under consideration were Judaizers (the circumcision). As such, they possessed a prejudiced preference for the Law, boasting of their privileges as sons of Moses. Their Jewish fables and commandments of men were proclaimed to turn believers from the truth (verse 14) as well as to build a base of support for their greedy lifestyles. Paul, in depicting these money-loving propagators of error, quotes Epimenides of Gnossus, a poet who lived in 600 B.C., saying, "The Cretians are always liars, evil beasts and slow bellies." Since Paul states that this witness concerning these loafers was true, what did he mean? The very word "kretizein" or "to Cretize" meant "to deceive" or "to utter a lie." They were also "evil beasts," a description of their brutal natures. Furthermore, they were called "slow bellies," a derogatory term used to describe their laziness created by excessive fleshly practices which drained their energies.

The Holy Spirit, through Paul, demands that such greedy sluggards be rebuked in order that they might become *sound in the faith* (verse 13), or literally that they might begin proclaiming and practicing pure doctrine which leads to a God-honoring lifestyle (see 2 Corinthians 5:17).

Adam Clarke states, "This crowd was to be rebuked cuttingly and severely because of their crimes which consisted of despising the truth and teaching others to do the same."

While some fundamentalists classify this

crowd as brothers, I cannot, because Titus 1:16, describing them, declares, *They profess that they know God; but in works they deny him, being abominable, and disobedient, and unto every good work reprobate.* Since Revelation 21:8 proves that the abominable are eternally incarcerated in the lake of fire, and since the "false teachers" are described as abominable, I classify them as apostates in my listing.

10. DON'T RECEIVE THEM. *For many deceivers are entered into the world, who confess not that Jesus Christ is come in the flesh. This is a deceiver and an antichrist. Look to yourselves, that we lose not those things which we have wrought, but that we receive a full reward. Whosoever transgresseth, and abideth not in the doctrine of Christ, hath not God. He that abideth in the doctrine of Christ, he hath both the Father and the Son. If there come any unto you, and bring not this doctrine, receive him not into your house, neither bid him God speed: for he that biddeth him God speed is partaker of his evil deeds* (2 John 7-11).

John deals sternly with apostates and apostasy in this text. However, it is important to remember that *all scripture is given by inspiration of God* (2 Timothy 3:16). Thus, the Holy Spirit is literally speaking through the beloved apostle. With this in mind, 1 John 2:22 states,

Who is a liar but he that denieth that Jesus is the Christ? He is antichrist, that denieth the Father and the Son. Shedding further light on the subject, 2 John 7 adds, [Apostates] *confess not that Jesus Christ is come in the flesh* [that God became man or the God-man.] Hence they are again called "deceivers and antichrists."

Now what should be the believer's relationship to "false teachers," "apostates," "liars," "deceivers" and "antichrists?" Should he enlist their support? Should he allow them to conduct a church service or home Bible study group? Absolutely not. Their transgression and rejection of the "doctrine of Christ" proves that they have not God (see verse 9). Therefore, *receive him not into your house, neither bid him God speed* [saying "God bless you" to them] (verse 10). Why not? *For he that biddeth him God speed is partaker of his evil deeds* (verse 11). Since the catastrophic judgment for aiding and abetting apostate teachers is the loss of rewards at the Judgment Seat of Christ (2 John 8 and 2 Corinthians 5:10,11), DON'T RECEIVE THEM. It's not worth it.

The texts presented to this point have been conscientiously interpreted in their contextual settings. Sixty-five of the greatest theological minds have been extremely beneficial in confirming my convictions regarding these texts.

There should not be one iota of doubt as to "separatism's" scriptural base concerning apostasy. However, may I add a note of caution once again. While it is true that we must "come out from," "judge," "identify," "withdraw from," "turn away from," "receive not," and "rebuke" apostates, we must also "avoid," "reprove," and "mark" immoral men whose *eyes* [are] *full of adultery* (2 Peter 2:14), whose mouths are full of *filthiness...foolish talking* [and] *jesting* (Ephesians 5:4) and whose hands covetously reach out greedily for gain. They also are defectors from righteousness, having turned away from the doctrine of godliness. *No whoremonger, nor unclean person, nor covetous man, who is an idolater, hath any inheritance in the kingdom of Christ and of God. Be not ye therefore partakers with them* (Ephesians 5:5,7).

Fundamentalism's separatist position on brothers

In concluding this study on separatism, we will analyze three final texts that deal with brothers in Christ. A World Congress of Fundamentalists, drew up the following listing under the heading: "Separation from disobedient saints and appeasers."

A. *Note that man* (2 Thessalonians 3:14)
B. *Withdraw yourself* (2 Thessalonians 3:6)
C. *Have no company with* (2 Thessalonians 3:14)
D. *Rebuke them sharply* (Titus 1:13)

115

E. *Count him not* [as] *an enemy* (2 Thessalonians 3:15)
F. *Admonish him as a brother* (2 Thessalonians 3:15)
G. Keep not company (1 Corinthians 5:11)
H. *With such an one no not to eat* (1 Corinthians 5:11)

Then they added, "And while adhering to this separatist position, we will *let brotherly love continue*" (Hebrews 13:1).

Are you impressed by this eight-point listing? Don't be. It amounts to little when analyzed and interpreted. Notice that points A, B, C, E, and F are all from the same portion of scripture. Points G and H are based upon one verse. Last but not least, point D does not belong in this grouping. Look again under apostasy, point 9 of this chapter, to understand why.

Basically then, two texts have been used to create the greatest mistrust of brothers in the history of Christendom. This tragedy exists because a platform and position has been built upon an erroneous interpretation of God's Word.

For years I, as a young man, accepted the above guidelines without question. Finally, I saw the inconsistency and inaccuracy of what I had swallowed. All it produces is bigotry, prejudice, and a condemnation of numerous innocent brothers. Presently, many fundamentalists are beginning to realize that something is drastically wrong within the movement. The grieved consciences of these brothers will not allow them to remain silent.

They, too, are grieved over the "war games" the neo-fundamentalist leadership seemingly enjoys playing. They care not how many of their own troops are wounded or injured. Nor do they mind continuing the battle based upon misunderstood or misinterpreted texts. As long as recruits continue to obediently follow their commands, the fighting must continue.

At this point, I feel compelled to describe the method of operation used to either humiliate or ex-communicate fellow brothers in Christ. It is the "trickle down" theory, whereby men and movements become guilty by association. If a fundamentalist shares a speaking engagement or time of fellowship with the friend of a friend of a friend of a pseudo-fundamentalist, who fellowshipped with a neo-evangelical, he becomes guilty of compromise. Then all who fellowship with the newly discovered traitor are also placed on an observation list. Thus, the witch-hunt never ceases. Is the situation really that absurd? You be the judge.

In a 35-page release, Dr. D. J. attempts to discredit scores of men and movements based upon his opinions and misinterpretations of Scripture. Note his "guilty by association," trickle-down theory in all of its splendor. He states, "Dr. Van Impe's ties with the new evangelical Trans-World Radio ministry were boldly declared by Dr. Paul Freed, president of Trans-World Radio, when Dr. Van Impe appeared on a nationwide TV special promoting the Trans-World Radio work."

Question: "Why are Dr. Paul Freed and the Trans-World Radio network condemned as new-evangelicals?

Dr. J: "'The Daily Word,' the Trans-World Radio devotional guide, contains full page pictures of three well-known religious leaders: Dr. Theodore Epp, Dr. J. Vernon McGee, and Dr. Jack Van Impe. Dr. Van Impe permitted his picture to be displayed twice on the same page with two well-known religious new-evangelical leaders."

Question: "Why are Drs. McGee and Epp new-evangelicals?"

[I will only take space to trace Dr. Epp's supposed downfall —JVI]

Dr. J: Dr. Theodore Epp allowed Dr. Dave Breese to be a guest speaker on his program. Also, in its publication, *The Good News Broadcaster,* Back to the Bible featured a picture of the ideal family. In it the father had mod hair. Hence, Back to the Bible is certainly turning away from the Bible.

Question: "Why is Dr. David Breese suspect?"

118

Dr. J: "Dr. Dave Breese was chairman of the 1977 convention of the National Association of Evangelicals."

Thus Dr. Breese is guilty because of his association with the NAE, and Dr. Epp is guilty because of his friendship with Dr. Breese, and Dr. Freed is guilty because of allowing Dr. Epp to use TWR facilities, and Jack Van Impe is guilty for using the station that airs the programs of Drs. McGee and Epp, as well as permitting his picture to appear in the same brochure with them!

Are you convinced after reading this analysis of "men and movements," by one who practices and promotes the "rules" of a "World Congress of Fundamentalists," that Jack Van Impe is a fellow traveler with apostates? Have I become such because I proclaim Christ to the world via the facilities of Trans-World Radio, a God-honoring ministry led by one of the greatest Christians I have ever known—Dr. Paul Freed? Is he tainted because he allows Dr. Theodore Epp to use TWR facilities to also proclaim Christ to the world? Is the honorable Dr. Epp religiously soiled because he allowed Dr. Dave Breese to be guest speaker on his Christ-exalting program? Is Dr. Breese a fellow traveler with apostates because he chaired the 1977 conference of the National Association of Evangelicals 17 years ago? Enough is enough! The witch-hunt must cease.

The situation is heartbreaking, especially when one realizes that such a condemnatory stand against brothers in Christ is based upon three misinterpreted biblical texts.

1. First Corinthians 5:11. Keep not company. *But now I have written unto you not to keep company, if any man that is called a brother be a fornicator, or covetous, or an idolater, or a railer, or a drunkard, or an extortioner; with such an one no not to eat.*

There is no doubt that God wants "brothers in Christ" to separate from other "brothers in Christ," when this form of withdrawal is beneficial to the erring believer's restoration. However, our congresses and conferences on fundamentalism have failed to see who the fallen are. They are not brothers who sat in the wrong pew at the wrong time but rather:

> **A. Fornicators**—those who practice pre-marital sex, adultery, homosexuality, or any other fleshly deviation.
> **B. The Covetous**—those whose lives are lived for monetary gain. Greed for materialism depicts them. They attempt to get all they can, any way they can.

C. Idolaters—those whose souls' devotion is given over to any object that usurps the place of God in their lives.

D. Railers—those who revile or scold in harsh, insolent, or abusive language. Dr. H. A. Ironside states, "A railer is a person who has a tongue loose at both ends and a pivot in the middle, a vicious talker, an evil speaker, one who can destroy the reputation of another just as a murderer drives a dagger into the heart and destroys a life. A character assassin is as wicked in the sight of God as a murderer.

E. Drunkards (self-explanatory)

F. Extortioners—those who illegally take things from others. They force their victims to give them objects that are not due them or that are not rightfully theirs.

After studying this text, how in the name of rationality can the command to "keep not company" apply to any brother in Christ who shakes hands with the third cousin of a compromiser?

Many years ago, Dr. M. R. DeHaan had it right when he said (perhaps prophetically), "This Corinthian crowd was so busy fighting, bickering, envying one another, splitting theological hairs, and arguing over personalities, ordinances, and doctrines that they paid no attention to the terrible immoral situation in their midst."

Brothers, let's obey God's Word without question, but let's at least base our conviction on what the verse teaches. Then we'll get back to our historic fundamentalist roots.

2. Second Thessalonians 3:6-15. This Congress of Fundamentalists listed five points under this one text. They are:

A. *Note that man* (verse 14).
B. *Withdraw yourselves* (verse 6).
C. *Have no company with* (verse 14).
D. *Count him not as an enemy* (verse 15).
E. *Admonish him as a brother* (verse 15).

The interpretation by some errant fundamentalists of the inerrant Word of God concerning this text is that the "disorderly" are "brothers" who fellowshipped with brothers, who fellowshipped with disobedient brothers who had been disfellowshipped because of compromise. Not one of my 65 theological sources would accept this interpretation. Let's look at the text in context.

Now we command you, brethren, in the name of our Lord Jesus

Christ, that ye withdraw yourselves from every brother that walketh disorderly, and not after the tradition which he received of us.

For yourselves know how ye ought to follow us: for we behaved not ourselves disorderly among you; neither did we eat any man's bread for nought; but wrought with labour and travail night and day, that we might not be chargeable to any of you: not because we have not power, but to make ourselves an ensample unto you to follow us. For even when we were with you, this we commanded you, that if any would not work, neither should he eat. For we hear that there are some which walk among you disorderly, working not at all, but are busybodies.

Now them that are such we command and exhort by our Lord Jesus Christ, that with quietness they work, and eat their own bread. But ye, brethren, be not weary in well doing. And if any man obey not our word by this epistle, note that man, and have no company with him, that he may be ashamed. Yet count him not as an enemy, but admonish him as a brother.

Who are the disorderly then? The text in context speaks for itself. Nevertheless, let's use quotes from past and present theological giants to enforce the truth.

Dr. Adam Clarke: "The disorderly were those who were not working. They were either lounging at home or becoming religious gossips. They were busybodies doing everything they should not be doing, impertinent meddlers in other people's business; prying into other people's affairs, magnifying or minifying, mistaking or underrating everything. They were newsmongers and telltales—an abominable race and a curse to every neighborhood they settled."

Dr. Charles Ellicott: "They worked not at all, but were busybodies. This is what constituted their disorderliness. They also held gossiping discussions."

Dr. Marvin Vincent: "They were idlers. Have no company with them."

Dr. John Walvoord: "Some had adopted the philosophy that the world owed them a living. Well, *if any would not work, neither should he eat* (2 Thessalonians 3:10). The very fact that they were idle led them into all sorts of difficulty. Idleness is fertile ground in which the devil can sow seeds. So Paul's exhortation was 'Get busy. Earn an honest living. Pay your own way. Take care of yourself. You will not have time then to be interfering with other people's business and making a nuisance of yourself.'"

Dr. A. Gabelein: "The disorder defined by the remainder of the context is loafing. This was contrary to the teaching (tradition) that Paul had given them earlier. The reluctant idler was not to be treated as an enemy, cut off from all contacts, but was allowed to continue in a brotherly status. It was social ostracism first, then 1 Corinthians 5:9-11."

Dr. Albert Barnes: "Paul warned in 1 Thessalonians 4:11 that believers were to *study to be quiet, and to do* [their] *own business, and to work with* [their] *own hands.* This was the tradition they had learned from Paul and were commanded to keep. If they did not obey this command, they were to be noted, and one's company was to be denied them." [see 2 Thessalonians 3:6,14 —JVI.]

Wycliffe Commentary: "They were disorderly or unruly as described in 1 Thessalonians 5:14. They did not follow tradition—Paul's personal example concerning work (see 2 Thessalonians 2:15 and 1 Thessalonians 4:11,12). It was an attack on laziness."

Dr. H. A. Ironside: "These men to whom Paul refers were simply ignoring the divine plan for work. When men are not employed properly they busy themselves in matters in which they should not interfere. So they became a nuisance and were used of Satan. The tongue does not offend so seriously when the hands are kept busy."

If you have not discovered who the "disorderly" are at this juncture, you never will. Needless to say, they are not pseudo-fundamentalists. Who are they then? Read the text again. Then practice scriptural separation.

As I bring this message to its summation, I must insert a third point that deals with brothers. Usually this portion of Scripture is listed under the heading of "apostasy" within fundamentalist ranks. However, I believe it comes under the heading of "brothers in Christ.

3. Titus 3:10. REJECT THEM.
A man that is a heretic after the first and second admonition, reject.

A HERETIC CLASSIFIED AS A BROTHER? Yes. Why? Read on.

Dr. Albert Barnes presents us with a startling twist as to the interpretation of this text. He says, "The word *heretic* is now commonly applied to one who holds to some fundamental error or doctrine (the dictionary definition rather than the original Greek). Originally, then, it meant 'one who is a promoter of a sect or party; the man who makes divisions instead of aiming to promote unity.' Such a man may form sects and parties on some points of doctrine on which he differs from others or on some custom, religious rite, or peculiar practice. He may make some **unimportant matter** a ground of distinction from his brethren and may **refuse fellow-ship** with them and start a new organization."

If the above interpretation is accurate—and Drs. Jamieson, Faucett, Brown, Black, Rowley, Ellicott, Guthrie, Motyer, Stibbs, Wiseman, Clark, Vine, Ironside, and Henry agree that it is—then **true separatists** should **separate** from **factious separatists** who separate from all those who will not bow to their **man-made separatist issues!**

How true. Presently, we fight and fuss over men, movements, and ministries. One can build a following by taking a stand against hair styles, clothing fashions, music preferences, slide presentations, Christian ventriloquists, puppets, gospel magicians, chalk talks, yo-yo demonstrations, karate exhibitions, Bible plays, story tellers, religious talk shows, discussion groups, quiz programs, and Sunday school contests—all classified as *gimmicks*.

Those who lead such anti-demonstrations might just be the "heretics" God tells us to reject. God's aim is UNITY (Ephesians 4:1-3). Let's work at it as we reject those who reject the above gifted men and the diversified ministries God has given them to use for His glory.

When divisive leaders erect organizations on "heretical premises," (New Testament definition) centered around **unimportant matters,** the results are predictable. They soon turn against each other and devour one another. Could this be the reason that **three fundamentalist groups** either passed resolutions or censured one another at their conferences? Let's get back to the Scriptures and rebuild a biblical movement.

To help build this unity, I give you another set of "thems" that God gave to me after spending 100 hours in prayer, meditation, and research for this chapter.

WHAT ABOUT OUR OBEDIENCE TO THIS FINAL LISTING OF "THEMS"? THEY, TOO, ARE IN GOD'S INSPIRED, INERRANT WORD.

1. BE RECONCILED TO THEM (Matthew 5:24).
2. BE KINDLY AFFECTIONED TOWARD THEM (Romans 12:10).
3. PREFER THEM (Romans 12:10).
4. REJOICE WITH THEM (Romans 12:15).
5. WEEP WITH THEM (Romans 12:15).
6. BE OF THE SAME MIND TOWARD THEM (Romans 12:16).
7. LIVE PEACEABLY WITH THEM (Romans 12:18).
8. DON'T JUDGE THEM (Romans 14:10).

9. DESTROY THEM NOT (Romans 14:15).
10. PLEASE THEM (Romans 15:2).
11. BE LIKEMINDED TOWARD THEM (Romans 15:5).
12. RECEIVE THEM (Romans 15:7).
13. ADMONISH THEM (Romans 15:14).
14. SALUTE THEM WITH AN HOLY KISS (Romans 16:16).
15. CARE FOR THEM (1 Corinthians 12:25).
16. RESTORE THEM (Galatians 6:1).
17. BEAR THEM AND THEIR BURDENS (Galatians 6:2).
18. DO GOOD TO THEM (Galatians 6:10).
19. FORBEAR THEM (Colossians 3:13).
20. SPEAK NOT EVIL OF THEM (James 4:11,12).
21. PRAY FOR THEM (James 5:16).
22. HAVE COMPASSION FOR THEM (1 Peter 3:8).
23. SHOW BROTHERLY KINDNESS TO THEM (2 Peter 1:7).

24. LOVE THEM (1 John 3:14; 4:7,8).
25. DIE FOR THEM (1 John 3:16).

I have but skimmed God's commandments on kindness. There are approximately three hundred additional verses on love. *This is the way, walk ye in it* (Isaiah 30:21). For *If we walk in the light, as he is in the light, we have fellowship one with another* (1 John 1:7).

Chapter 9

Obeying Man or God

Let us therefore follow after the things which make for peace, and things wherewith one may edify another (Romans 14:19).

In the light of what has already been said, may I appeal to all loving fundamentalists and evangelicals to make a decision this day as to what is right and wrong. Study once again the two misinterpreted texts in chapter eight. Then consider the scores of verses presented in this chapter. There can be only two courses of action: you must either choose to continue bowing to the man-made misinterpretations of the Bible, or obey approximately three hundred of God's plain commandments to fellowship with and love the brethren. The following verses need no explanation. Simply read, believe, and obey them:

I. Dissension among brothers
Luke 17:3,4: *If thy brother trespass against thee, rebuke him; and if he repent, forgive him.*

And if he trespass against thee seven times in a day, and seven times in a day turn again to thee, saying, I repent; thou shalt forgive him.

Romans 14:19: *Let us therefore follow after the things which make for peace, and things wherewith one may edify another.*

First Corinthians 1:10: *Now I beseech you, brethren, by the name of our Lord Jesus Christ, that ye all speak the same thing, and that there be no divisions among you; but that ye be perfectly joined together in the same mind and in the same judgment. For it hath been declared unto me of you, my brethren, by them which are of the house of Chloe, that there are contentions among you.*

First Corinthians 3:1-4: *And I, brethren, could not speak unto you as unto spiritual, but as unto carnal, even as unto babes in Christ. I have fed you with milk, and not with meat: for hitherto ye were not able to bear it, neither yet now are ye able. For ye are yet carnal: for whereas there is among you envying, and strife, and divisions, are ye not carnal, and walk as men? For while one saith, I am of Paul; and another, I am of Apollos, are ye not carnal?*

First Corinthians 11:17,18: *Ye come together not for the better, but for the worse...there be divisions among you.*

The result of the contentions of 1 Corinthians 1:11 and 11:17 are described in 1 Corinthians 11:27-33, *Wherefore whosoever shall eat this bread, and drink this cup of the Lord, unworthily, shall be guilty of the body and blood of the Lord. But let a man examine himself, and so let him eat of that bread, and drink of that cup. For he that eateth and drinketh unworthily, eateth and drinketh damnation to himself, not discerning the Lord's body. For this cause many are weak and sickly among you, and many sleep. For if we would judge ourselves, we should not be judged. But when we are judged, we are chastened of the Lord, that we should not be condemned with the world. Wherefore, my brethren, when ye come together to eat, tarry one for another.*

Colossians 3:13: *Forbearing one another, and forgiving one another, if any man have a quarrel against any: even as Christ forgave you, so also do ye.*

Philippians 4:2: *Be of the same mind in the Lord.*

First Timothy 3:3: [A minister is to be] *patient, not a brawler, not covetous.*

Second Timothy 2:24: *The servant of the Lord must not strive; but be gentle unto all men.*

Hebrews 12:14,15: *Follow peace with all men, and holiness, without which no man shall see the Lord: looking diligently lest any man fail of the grace of God; lest any root of bitterness springing up trouble you, and thereby many be defiled.*

James 1:26: *If any man among you seem to be religious, and bridleth not his tongue, but de-*

133

ceiveth his own heart, this man's religion is vain.

James 3:2: *If any man offend not in word, the same is a perfect man, and able also to bridle the whole body.*

James 4:1: *From whence come wars and fightings among you? come they not hence, even of your lusts that war in your members?*

James 4:11,12: *Speak not evil one of another, brethren...who art thou that judgest another?*

II. Fellowship with brothers

Mark 9:38-42: *And John answered him, saying, Master, we saw one casting out devils in thy name, and he followeth not us: and we forbad him, because he followeth not us. But Jesus said, Forbid him not... For he that is not against us is on our part. For whosoever shall give you a cup of water to drink in my name, because ye belong to Christ, verily I say unto you, he shall not lose his reward. And whosoever shall offend one of these little ones that believe in me, it is better for him that a millstone were hanged about his neck, and he were cast into the sea.*

Luke 9:49-56: *And John answered and said, Master, we saw one casting out devils in thy name; and we forbad him, because he followeth not with us. And Jesus said unto him, Forbid him not: for he that is not against us is for us. And it came to pass, when the time was come that he should be received up, he stedfastly set* *his face to go to Jerusalem, and sent messengers before his face: and they went, and entered into a village of the Samaritans, to make ready for him. And they did not receive him, because his face was as though he would go to Jerusalem. And when his disciples James and John saw this, they said, Lord, wilt thou that we command fire to come down from heaven, and consume them, even as Elias did? But he turned, and rebuked them, and said, Ye know not what manner of spirit ye are of. For the Son of man is not come to destroy men's lives, but to save them.*

Luke 11:42: *For ye tithe mint and rue and all manner of herbs, and pass over judgment and the love of God.*

John 6:37: *Him that cometh to me I will in no wise cast out.*

John 10:16: *And other sheep I have, which are not of this fold: them also I must bring, and they shall hear my voice; and there shall be one fold, and one shepherd.*

John 17:21-23: *That they all may be one...even as we are one...that they may be made perfect in one.*

Galatians 2:4-6,11-14: *False brethren...came in privily to spy out our liberty which we have in Christ Jesus, that they might bring us into bondage: To whom we gave place by subjection, no, not for an hour; that the truth of the gospel might continue...for they who seemed to be somewhat in conference added nothing...But when*

135

Peter was come to Antioch, I withstood him to the face, because he was to be blamed. For before that certain came from James, he did eat with the Gentiles: but when they were come, he withdrew and separated himself, fearing them which were of the circumcision. And the other Jews dissembled likewise with him; insomuch that Barnabas also was carried away with their dissimulation. But when I saw that they walked not uprightly according to the truth of the gospel, I said unto Peter before them all, If thou, being a Jew, livest after the manner of Gentiles, and not as do the Jews, why compellest thou the Gentiles to live as do the Jews?

Galatians 5:1: *Stand fast therefore in the liberty wherewith Christ hath made us free, and be not entangled again with the yoke of bondage.*

Philippians 1:15-18: *Some indeed preach Christ even of envy and strife; and some also of good will: The one preach Christ of contention, not sincerely, supposing to add affliction to my bonds: But the other of love, knowing that I am set for the defence of the gospel. What then? notwithstanding, every way, whether in pretence, or in truth, Christ is preached; and I therein do rejoice, yea, and will rejoice.*

First John 1:7: *But if we walk in the light, as he is in the light, we have fellowship one with another, and the blood of Jesus Christ his Son cleanseth us from all sin.*

Revelation 5:9,10: *For* [Christ] *wast slain, and*

hast redeemed us to God by thy blood out of every kindred, and tongue, and people, and nation; and hast made us unto our God kings and priests.

III. Love one another

A. Love for our brothers

We are not to be angry with our brothers. Why?

Matthew 5:22: *Whosoever is angry with his brother without a cause shall be in danger of the judgment: and whosoever shall say to his brother, Raca, shall be in danger of the council: but whosoever shall say, Thou fool, shall be in danger of hell fire.*

John 13:34,35: *A new commandment I give unto you, That ye love one another; as I have loved you, that ye also love one another. By this shall all men know that ye are my disciples, if ye have love one to another.*

John 15:9,10,17: *Continue ye in my love. If ye keep my commandments, ye shall abide in my love.... These things I command you, that ye love one another.*

Romans 12:10,16,21: *Be kindly affectioned one to another with brotherly love; in honour preferring one another. Be of the same mind one toward another. Mind not high things, but condescend to men of low estate. Be not wise in*

137

your own conceits. Be not overcome of evil, but overcome evil with good.

Romans 13:7,8: *Render therefore to all their dues: tribute to whom tribute is due; custom to whom custom; fear to whom fear; honour to whom honour. Owe no man any thing, but to love one another: for he that loveth another hath fulfilled the law.*

In the following texts, *charity* is synonymous or another term for *love.*

First Corinthians 13:1-7,13: *Though I speak with the tongues of men and of angels, and have not charity, I am become as sounding brass, or a tinkling cymbal. And though I have the gift of prophecy, and understand all mysteries, and all knowledge; and though I have all faith, so that I could remove mountains, and have not charity, I am nothing. And though I bestow all my goods to feed the poor, and though I give my body to be burned, and have not charity, it profiteth me nothing. Charity suffereth long, and is kind; charity envieth not; charity vaunteth not itself, is not puffed up, doth not behave itself unseemly, seeketh not her own, is not easily provoked, thinketh no evil; rejoiceth not in iniquity, but rejoiceth in the truth; beareth all things, believeth all things, hopeth all things, endureth all things. And now abideth faith, hope, charity, these three; but the greatest of these is charity.*

First Corinthians 14:1: *Follow after charity, and desire spiritual gifts.*

First Corinthians 16:14: *Let all your things be done with charity.*

Galatians 5:13: *Use not liberty for an occasion to the flesh, but by love serve one another.*

Ephesians 3:17-19: [Be] *rooted and grounded in love* [that you] *may be able to comprehend with all saints what is the breadth, and length, and depth, and height; And to know the love of Christ, which passeth knowledge, that ye might be filled with all the fulness of God.*

Ephesians 4:1-3,15,16: *Walk worthy of the vocation wherewith ye are called, with all lowliness and meekness, with longsuffering, forbearing one another in love; endeavouring to keep the unity of the Spirit in the bond of peace.* [Speak] *the truth in love,* [that you] *may grow up into him in all things, which is the head, even Christ: from whom the whole body fitly joined together and compacted by that which every joint supplieth, according to the effectual working in the measure of every part, maketh increase of the body unto the edifying of itself in love.*

Ephesians 5:2: *Walk in love, as Christ also hath loved us, and hath given himself for us an offering and a sacrifice to God.*

Philippians 1:9: [Let] *your love...abound yet more and more in knowledge and in all judgment.*

Philippians 2:2: *Be likeminded, having the same love, being of one accord, of one mind.*

Colossians 1:4,7,8: *Love...all the saints...*[be] *a faithful minister of Christ...*[declare]*...your love in the Spirit.*

Colossians 2:2: [Let your heart] *be comforted... knit together in love, and unto all riches of the full assurance of understanding.*

Colossians 3:14: *Put on charity, which is the bond of perfectness.*

First Thessalonians 3:12,13: *Increase and abound in love one toward another, and toward all men...stablish your hearts unblameable in holiness before God.*

First Thessalonians 4:9: *Love one another.*

First Thessalonians 5:8: [Put] *on the breast-plate of faith and love.*

Second Thessalonians 1:3: [Let] *the charity of every one of you all toward each other* [abound].

Second Thessalonians 3:5: *Direct your hearts into the love of God.*

First Timothy 1:5: *Now the end of the commandment is charity out of a pure heart, and of a good conscience, and of faith unfeigned.*

First Timothy 4:12: *Be thou an example of the believers, in word, in conversation, in charity.*

First Timothy 6:11: *Follow after righteousness, godliness, faith, love, patience, meekness.*

Second Timothy 2:22: *Follow righteousness, faith, charity, peace, with them that call on the Lord out of a pure heart.*

Second Timothy 3:10,14: *Fully* [know]*... doctrine...purpose, faith, longsuffering, charity,*

140

patience...[and] *continue thou in the things which thou hast learned and hast been assured of.*

Titus 1:7,8,14: *A bishop must be blameless...not selfwilled, not soon angry...a lover of good men ...Not giving heed to...commandments of men, that turn from the truth.*

Ministers, especially, are to:

Titus 2:1,2: *Speak...the things which become sound doctrine: that aged men be sober, grave, temperate, sound in faith, in charity, in patience.*
Titus 3:1-3:*Be subject to principalities and powers...obey magistrates...ready to every good work...speak evil of no man...be no brawlers, but gentle, showing all meekness unto all men. For we ourselves also were sometimes foolish, disobedient, deceived, serving divers lusts and pleasures, living in malice and envy, hateful, and hating one another.*

The Spirit of God again admonishes us to:

Hebrews 13:1: *Let brotherly love continue.*
First Peter 1:22: [Purify our] *souls in obeying the truth...unto unfeigned love of the brethren* [and]*...love one another with a pure heart.*
First Peter 2:17: *Honour all men. Love the brotherhood.*
First Peter 3:8,9: *Be ye all of one mind, having compassion one of another, love as brethren... Not rendering evil for evil, or railing for railing: but contrariwise blessing.*
First Peter 4:8: *Above all things have fervent*

[love] *among yourselves: for* [love] *shall cover the multitude of sins.*

First Peter 5:14: *Greet...one another with a kiss of* [love].

Second Peter 1:5-8: *Add to your faith virtue; and to virtue knowledge; and to knowledge temperance; and to temperance patience; and to patience godliness; and to godliness brotherly kindness; and to brotherly kindness* [love]. *For if these things be in you, and abound, they make you that ye shall neither be barren nor unfruitful.*

Further scriptural instruction tells us that:

First John 2:9-11: *He that saith he is in the light, and hateth his brother, is in darkness even until now. He that loveth his brother abideth in the light, and there is none occasion of stumbling in him. But he that hateth his brother is in darkness, and walketh in darkness, and knoweth not wither he goeth, because that darkness hath blinded his eyes.*

First John 3:10,11,14-18: *In this the children of God are manifest, and the children of the devil: whosoever doeth not righteousness is not of God, neither he that loveth not his brother. For this is the message that ye heard from the beginning, that we should love one another. We know that we have passed from death unto life, because we love the brethren. He that loveth not his brother abideth in death. Whosoever hateth his brother is a murderer: and ye know that no murderer* *hath eternal life abiding in him. Hereby perceive we the love of God, because he laid down his life for us: and we ought to lay down our lives for the brethren. But whoso hath this world's good, and seeth his brother have need, and shutteth up his bowels of compassion from him, how dwelleth the love of God in him? My little children, let us not love in word, neither in tongue; but in deed and in truth.*

First John 3:23: *And this is his commandment, That we should believe on the name of his Son Jesus Christ, and love one another, as he gave us commandment.*

First John 4:7,8: *Beloved, let us love one another: for love is of God; and every one that loveth is born of God, and knoweth God. He that loveth not knoweth not God; for God is love.*

First John 4:10-12,16,20,21: *Herein is love, not that we loved God, but that he loved us, and sent his Son to be the propitiation for our sins. Beloved, if God so loved us, we ought also to love one another...If we love one another, God dwelleth in us, and his love is perfected in us...God is love; and he that dwelleth in love dwelleth in God, and God in him. If a man say, I love God, and hateth his brother, he is a liar: for he that loveth not his brother whom he hath seen, how can he love God whom he hath not seen? And this commandment have we from* *him, That he who loveth God love his brother also.*

First John 5:2: *By this we know that we love the children of God, when we love God, and keep his commandments.*

Second John 5: *And now I beseech thee...love one another.*

Jude 21: *Keep yourselves in the love of God.*

Matthew 12:50: *Whosoever shall do the will of my Father which is in heaven, the same is my brother.*

Mark 3:35: *Whosoever shall do the will of God, the same is my brother.*

B. Love for our neighbors

Matthew 19:19: *Thou shalt love thy neighbour as thyself.*

Matthew 22:39: *Thou shalt love thy neighbour as thyself.*

Mark 12:30,31: *Thou shalt love the Lord thy God with all thy heart, and with all thy soul, and with all thy mind, and with all thy strength: this is the first commandment. And the second is like, namely this, Thou shalt love thy neighbour as thyself. There is none other commandment greater than these.*

Romans 13:9,10: *Thou shalt love thy neighbour as thyself. Love worketh no ill to his neighbour: therefore love is the fulfilling of the law.*

Galatians 5:14: *For all the law is fulfilled in*

*one word, even in this; Thou shalt love thy neigh-
bour as thyself.*

James 2:8: *If ye fulfill the royal law according
to the scripture, Thou shalt love thy neighbour
as thyself.*

C. Love even for our enemies

Matthew 5:44-46: *Love your enemies, bless them
that curse you, do good to them that hate you,
and pray for them which despitefully use you,
and persecute you; that ye may be the children
of your Father which is in heaven: for he maketh
his sun to rise on the evil and on the good, and
sendeth rain on the just and on the unjust. For if
ye love them which love you, what reward have
ye? do not even the publicans the same?*

Luke 6:27,28,35: *Love your enemies, do good
to them which hate you, bless them that curse
you, and pray for them which despitefully use
you...love ye your enemies, and do good, and
lend, hoping for nothing again; and your reward shall be great, and ye shall be the children
of the Highest: for he is kind unto the unthankful
and to the evil.*

Romans 12:14,17: *Bless them which persecute
you: bless, and curse not. Recompense to no
man evil for evil. Provide things honest in the
sight of all men.*

Galatians 6:10: *As we have therefore opportunity, let us do good unto all men, especially unto
them who are of the household of faith.*

First Thessalonians 5:14,15: *Be patient toward all men. See that none render evil for evil unto any man; but ever follow that which is good, both among yourselves, and to all men.*

IV. Make peace with our brothers

Psalm 34:14: *Seek peace, and pursue it.*

Matthew 5:9: *Blessed are the peacemakers: for they shall be called the children of God.*

Mark 9:50: *Have peace one with another.*

Luke 2:13,14: *And suddenly there was with the angel a multitude of the heavenly host praising God, and saying, Glory to God in the highest, and on earth peace, good will toward men.*

Romans 12:18: *Live peaceably with all men.*

Romans 14:19: *Follow after the things which make for peace, and things wherewith one may edify another.*

Second Corinthians 13:11: *Live in peace.*

Galatians 5:22,23,25: *The fruit of the Spirit is love, joy, peace, longsuffering, gentleness, goodness, faith, meekness, temperance. If we live in the Spirit, let us also walk in the Spirit.*

Ephesians 4:3: *Endeavoring to keep the unity of the Spirit in the bond of peace.*

Ephesians 6:23: *Peace be to the brethren, and love with faith.*

Colossians 3:15: *Let the peace of God rule in your hearts.*

First Thessalonians 5:13: *Be at peace among yourselves.*

146

Hebrews 12:14: *Follow peace with all men.*
James 3:17,18: *The wisdom that is from above is...peaceable. And the fruit of righteousness is sown in peace of them that make peace.*
First Peter 3:10-12: *Refrain* [thy] *tongue from evil, and* [thy] *lips that they speak no guile... eschew evil, and do good...seek peace, and ensue it. For the eyes of the Lord are over the righteous, and his ears are open unto their prayers: but the face of the Lord is against them that do evil.*
First Peter 5:14: *Greet ye one another with a kiss of charity. Peace be with you all that are in Christ Jesus.*
Second Peter 3:14: *Be diligent that ye may be found of him in peace, without spot, and blameless.*

V. Forgiveness of brothers

Look again at the Scripture's clear teaching on this matter:
Matthew 6:12: *Forgive* [your] *debtors.*
Matthew 18:21,22: *How oft shall my brother sin against me, and I forgive him? till seven times? Jesus saith...Until* **seventy** *times seven.*
Mark 11:25,26: *When ye stand praying, forgive, if ye have ought against any...if ye do not forgive, neither will your Father which is in heaven forgive your trespasses.*
Luke 6:37: *Forgive, and ye shall be forgiven.*

Luke 11:4: *Forgive every one that is indebted to* [you].

Luke 17:3,4: *If thy brother trespass against thee, rebuke him; and if he repent, forgive him. And if he trespass against thee seven times in a day, and seven times in a day turn again to thee, saying, I repent; thou shalt forgive him.*

Second Corinthians 2:7: *Ye ought rather to forgive.*

Ephesians 4:30-32: *Grieve not the holy Spirit of God...Let all bitterness, and wrath, and anger, and clamour, and evil speaking, be put away from you, with all malice: and be ye kind one to another, tenderhearted, forgiving one another, even as God for Christ's sake hath forgiven you.*

Colossians 3:12,13: *Put on therefore, as the elect of God, holy and beloved, bowels of mercies, kindness, humbleness of mind, meekness, longsuffering; forbearing one another, and forgiving one another.*

VI. Show meekness toward brothers

Zephaniah 2:3: [Show] *meekness.*

Matthew 5:5: *Blessed are the meek: for they shall inherit the earth.*

Matthew 11:28-30: *Come unto me, all ye that labour and are heavy laden, and I will give you rest. Take my yoke upon you, and learn of me; for I am meek and lowly in heart: and ye shall find rest unto your souls. For my yoke is easy, and my burden is light.*

First Peter 3:4: [Put on] *the ornament of a meek and quiet spirit, which is in the sight of God of great price.*
Galatians 6:1,2: *Brethren, if a man be overtaken in a fault, ye which are spiritual, restore such an one in the spirit of meekness; considering thyself, lest thou also be tempted. Bear ye one another's burdens, and so fulfil the law of Christ.*
First Timothy 6:11: *Follow after righteousness, godliness, faith, love, patience, meekness.*
Second Timothy 2:24,25: *The servant of the Lord must not strive; but be gentle unto all men, apt to teach...in meekness instructing those that oppose themselves.*

VII. Be longsuffering toward brothers

Second Corinthians 6:3,4,6: [Give] *no offense in any thing, that the ministry be not blamed: but in all things* [approve yourselves] *as the ministers of God, in much patience...by pureness, by knowledge, by longsuffering, by kindness...by love unfeigned.*
Ephesians 4:1,2: *Walk worthy of the vocation wherewith ye are called, with all lowliness and meekness, with longsuffering, forbearing one another in love.*
Colossians 1:10,11: *Walk worthy of the Lord unto all pleasing, being fruitful in every good work, and increasing in the knowledge of*

God...unto all patience and longsuffering with joyfulness.

Colossians 3:12,13: *Put on...bowels of mercies, kindness, humbleness of mind, meekness, long-suffering; forbearing one another, and forgiving one another.*

Second Timothy 3:10: *Fully* [know] *my doctrine...purpose, faith, longsuffering, charity, patience.*

Second Timothy 4:2: *Preach the word; be instant in season, out of season; reprove, rebuke, exhort with all longsuffering and doctrine.*

VIII. Do good to all brothers

Psalm 34:14: *Depart from evil, and do good.*

Psalm 37:27: *Do good; and dwell for evermore.*

Matthew 5:44: *Love your enemies, bless them that curse you, do good to them that hate you, and pray for them which despitefully use you, and persecute you.*

Luke 2:14: [Practice] *good will toward men.*

Luke 6:27: *Love your enemies, do good to them which hate you.*

Luke 6:35: *Love ye your enemies, and do good ...and your reward shall be great, and ye shall be the children of the Highest: for he is kind unto the unthankful and to the evil.*

Galatians 6:10: *Let us do good unto all men.*

Colossians 1:10: [Be] *fruitful in every good work.*

First Thessalonians 5:15: *Follow that which is good, both among yourselves, and to all men.*
Titus 2:7,8: [Show yourself] *a pattern of good works...that he that is of the contrary part may be ashamed, having no evil thing to say of you.*
Hebrews 10:24: *Consider one another to provoke unto love and to good works.*
James 3:17,18: [Seek] *wisdom that is from above...full of mercy and good fruits...the fruit of righteousness is sown in peace of them that make peace.*

First Peter 3:10,11: *He that will love life, and see good days...let him eschew evil, and do good.*

IX. Be kind to brothers
Romans 12:10: *Be kindly affectioned one to another with brotherly love.*
First Corinthians 13:4: *Charity suffereth long, and is kind.*
Second Corinthians 6:4-6: *In all things* [approve yourselves] *as the ministers of God...In stripes, in imprisonments, in tumults, in labours, in watchings, in fastings; by pureness, by knowledge, by longsuffering, by kindness.*
Ephesians 4:32: *Be ye kind one to another.*
Colossians 3:12: *Put on therefore, as the elect of God, holy and beloved, bowels of mercies, kindness.*
Second Peter 1:5-7: *Add to your faith virtue; and to virtue knowledge; and to knowledge tem-*

perance; and to temperance patience; and to patience godliness; and to godliness brotherly kindness.

X. Be gentle to brothers

Galatians 5:22,23: *The fruit of the Spirit is love, joy, peace, longsuffering, gentleness, goodness, faith, meekness, temperance: against such there is no law.*

First Thessalonians 2:7,8: *We were gentle among you...because ye were dear to us.*

Second Timothy 2:24: *The servant of the Lord must...be gentle unto all men.*

Titus 3:2: *Speak evil of no man...be no brawlers, but gentle.*

James 3:17: *The wisdom that is from above is ...gentle.*

XI. Admonish brothers

First Thessalonians 5:12: *Know them which labour among you, and are over you in the Lord, and admonish you.*

Second Thessalonians 3:15: *Admonish [your] brother.*

XII. Have compassion on brothers

First Peter 3:8: *Be ye all of one mind, having compassion one of another, love as brethren...be courteous.*

XIII. Pray for brothers

First Thessalonians 5:25: *Brethren, pray for us.*

James 5:16: *Pray one for another.*

When these many commands from God's Word have been effectively woven into a Christian life, the result is a tenderness of spirit that immediately identifies that individual as a child of God and a true servant of the Lord Jesus Christ. It reflects the fullness of the Spirit and speaks of Christian maturity. Frances R. Havergal describes this tenderness of spirit as "October Mellowness," and discusses its nature and work in an article by that title in the *Herald of His Coming*. May the following excerpt speak to your heart.

It is much easier to convince a human soul of its natural impurity than to convince it of its natural hardness, and utter destitution of heavenly and divine tenderness of spirit. The very essence of the Gospel is a divinely imparted tenderness and sweetness of spirit. Without this, even the strongest religious life is a misrepresentation of the true Christlife. Even among intensely religious people, nothing is more rare to find than a continuous, all-pervading spirit of tenderness.

Tenderness of spirit is preeminently divine. It is not the delicacy and soft sensibility of a mere gentle make-up of body and mind, which some persons naturally possess in a high degree. Neither is it the tenderness of mind and manner which results from high culture and beautiful social training, though these are very valuable in life.

But it is a supernatural work throughout the whole spiritual being. It is an exquisite interior fountain of God's own sweetness and tenderness of nature, opened up in the inner spirit to such a degree that it completely inundates the soul, overflowing all the mental faculties, and saturating with its sweet waters the manners, expressions, words, and tones of the voice: mellowing the will, softening the judgments, melting the affections, refining the manners and moulding the whole being after the image of Him who was infinitely meek and lowly in heart. It cannot be borrowed, or put on for special occasions. It is emphatically supernatural, and must flow out incessantly from the inner fountains of the life, and resembles having every atom of our being soaked in sweet oil.

Deep tenderness of spirit is the very soul and marrow of the Christlife. Without it, the most vigorous life of righteousness and good works, and rigid purity of morals, and missionary zeal, and profuse liberality, and ascetic self-denial, and the most blameless conduct—utterly fail to measure up to the Christlife unveiled in the New Testament.

It is impossible to see the infinite excellence and necessity of real heavenly tenderness of spirit unless it is specially revealed to us by the Holy Ghost. It takes a direct revelation from God to enable us to discern what is the very marrow and fatness of Christ's character, the inexpressible tenderness and gentleness of His nature which is always the heart inside of the heart, and soul within the soul, of the Christlife.

What specific gravity is to the planet, what beauty is to the rainbow, what perfume is to the rose, what marrow is to the bone, what rhythm is to poetry, what sublimity is to the ocean, what the pulse is to the heart, what harmony is to music, what heat is to the human body—all this and much more is what tenderness of spirit is to religion.

Without tenderness of spirit the most intensely righteous, religious life is like the image of God without His

155

beauty and attractiveness. It is possible to be very religious, and staunch, and perservering in all Christian duties, even to be sanctified, and be a brave defender and preacher of holiness, to be mathematically orthodox, and blameless in outward life, and very zealous in good works—and yet to be greatly lacking in tenderness of spirit, that all-subduing, all-melting love, which is the very cream and quintessence of Heaven, and which incessantly streamed out from the eyes and voice of the blessed Jesus.

Many religious people seem loaded with good fruits, but the fruit tastes green. It lacks flavor and October mellowness. There is a touch of vinegar in their sanctity. Their very purity has an icy coldness to it. They seem to have a baptism on them, but it is not composed of those sweet spices of cinnamon, and calamus, and cassia, which God told Moses to compound as a fragrant type of the real sweetness of the Holy Spirit. Their testimonies are straight and definite, but they lack the melting quality. Their prayers are intelligent, and strong and pointed, but they lack the heart-piercing pathos of the dying Jesus. The summer heat in them is lacking. They preach eloquently and explain with utmost nicety what is actual and original sin, and what is pardon and purity, but they lack the burning flame, that interior furnace of throbbing love that sighs and weeps and breaks down under the shivering heat of all-consuming love.

This all pervading tenderness of spirit is not a novitiate grace. It is not a product of April but of October.

No scene in the Bible opens up a greater vista into the tenderness of the spirit of Jesus, than where He stooped and wrote on the ground, as if His modest and loving heart did not want to hear the horrible account of evil. As we gaze on the soul of Jesus at that time, we see infinite politeness, both toward the accused and accusers; not a trace of unkindness or severity to either party. His whole manner and speech and disposition filled the whole air as with a very sea of refinement, gentleness and inexpressive sweetness of spirit.

This and similar acts of Jesus is like an opening between mountains, through which we look far off on an outspreading silver sea of love, whose every undulation presents a new phase

157

of unspeakable tenderness toward the poor sinner he came to save. Tenderness of spirit makes its home in the bosom of Jesus, and from that holy castle looks out upon all other creatures, good and bad, through the hopeful, pleading medium of the heart that was pierced on the cross. Tenderness of spirit is in divine sympathy with the poor and downtrodden and unfortunate and hated classes of mankind.

It feels for the poor or any that are the common butt of worldly scorn. Whenever it hears of any of these spoken of in a harsh and bitter way, it feels a dagger pierce its own heart and a tear of sympathy comes to its eye, and a piercing silent prayer ascends from it to that God who hears the sighing of the prisoner and the cries of the unfortunate. It feels all things from God's standpoint, and lives but to receive and transmit the spotless sympathies and affections of Jesus. It understands the words of the Holy Ghost, *Be ye...tenderhearted, forgiving one another* (Ephesians 4:32). Tenderness must be in our very nature, and forgiveness is but the behavior of that nature.

What a beautiful description of true Christianity—the outliving of *Christ in you* (Colossians 1:27). The potential of such a life is inherent within every born-again believer, yet few truly allow the blessed Holy Spirit to possess them so completely that the character and attitude of Christ are manifest in them.

Perhaps your heart was convicted as you studied the many instructions of God in this chapter. If so, why not surrender yourself anew to His leadership in your life. Make the following prayer your desire, today and forever:

"Heavenly Father, as Your child, I have fallen short of the image of Christ in so many ways. Forgive me. I recommit myself to You today, and seek the fulness of Your Spirit in my life. Help me put away all bitterness, criticism, envying, and selfishness, replacing them with the love, understanding, compassion, and tenderness of Your Son, my Saviour. I want to know and love others as He does—looking beyond their faults and seeing their needs. In Jesus' name I pray, Amen."